THE
YEAR 'ROUND
HOLIDAY
BOOK

it's a God thing!

Other books in the Young Women of Faith Library

The Lily Series
> *Here's Lily!*
> *Lily Robbins, M.D. (Medical Dabbler)*
> *Lily and the Creep*
> *Lily's Ultimate Party*
> *Ask Lily*
> *Lily the Rebel*
> *Lights, Action, Lily!*
> *Lily Rules!*
> *Rough & Rugged Lily*
> *Lily Speaks!*

Nonfiction
> *The Beauty Book*
> *The Body Book*
> *The Buddy Book*
> *The Best Bash Book*
> *The Blurry Rules Book*
> *The It's MY Life Book*
> *The Creativity Book*
> *The Uniquely Me Book*
> *The Values & Virtues Book*
> *Dear Diary: A Girl's Book of Devotions*
> *Girlz Want to Know*
> *NIV Young Women of Faith Bible*
> *YWOF Journal: Hey! This Is Me*
> *Take It from Me*

Young Women of Faith

THE YEAR 'ROUND HOLIDAY BOOK

it's a God thing!

Written by Nancy Rue
Illustrated by Lyn Boyer

Zonderkidz

Zonder**kidz**™

The children's group of Zondervan

www.zonderkidz.com

The Year 'Round Holiday Book
Copyright © 2002 by Women of Faith

Requests for information should be addressed to:

Zonderkidz, *Grand Rapids, Michigan 49530*

ISBN: 0–310–70256–9

Published in association with the literary agency of Alive Communications, Inc., 7680 Goddard Street, Suite 200, Colorado Springs, CO 80920.

Editor: Barbara J. Scott
Interior design: Michelle Lenger
Art direction: Michelle Lenger
Printed in the United States of America

02 03 04 05/ ❖ DC/5 4 3 2

Contents

Making Holidays Holy Days (Without Driving Everybody Nuts!)

Do this in remembrance of me.
1 Corinthians 11:24

Okay—time to be honest. How often do you look at the calendar to see how many school days there are until your next holiday? And how often does it matter to you what the holiday is, just as long as you get the day off?

Sure, you might like the Memorial Day picnic or the Veterans' Day parade, and maybe your mom bakes a cherry pie for Presidents' Day. But chances are, unless it's Christmas or Thanksgiving, you don't much care about the reason you get to sleep in!

However, there are some holidays that you might want to consider more carefully. Let's begin by looking at the word itself. *Holiday* is kind of a contraction—like *don't* for *do not*—for "holy day." Even though we now refer to practically any day we don't have to go to school as a holiday, originally holy days were just that—days for observing something holy, something that was of God.

Nowadays, some of those holy days, which started out being sacred (holy), have become secular (worldly). Christmas is a good example. This holy day, created to celebrate the birth of Christ, has now become pretty secular. Many people get so busy with cookies, elves, and reindeer that they barely give Jesus and the manger a passing thought. The same is true for Easter, with its bunnies and chicks and baskets of candy, and Halloween, which has become a celebration of all things creepy and scary and disgusting.

Not only that, some of the original holy days and seasons are no longer observed by many Christians. Ever heard of Epiphany or the Feast of Pentecost? Do you know what Advent is? (Hint: It isn't just a time for Christmas shopping.) And how about Lent? Are you thinking it might be that time of year when people give up stuff—like candy and gum, kind of like a diet before they hit the Easter basket? They aren't out-of-date holy days, noted only by those denominations that observe the church year. These special days are important for all Christians because they give us opportunities to remember and celebrate all the things God is in our lives.

Think what it would be like if you never had a day off from school—time to sit back and regroup and get revived for, well, more school. Holy days give us a chance to get juiced up about God so you can get out there and let God live in you and through you.

In this book, we'll take a look at five different holy days and seasons, starting with Advent, which is the spiritual preparation for Christmas. We'll explore Epiphany and then Lent, which is the spiritual preparation for Easter, before taking a look at the Feast of Pentecost. We'll even examine some holidays that aren't part of the church year but are important to us as Americans. We'll look at how all those holidays and seasons got started and how you can celebrate them in a sacred way that will bring you even closer to God—without driving your family whacko at the same time.

Notice that we aren't going to talk a lot about Christmas and Easter, because most families and churches have those pretty well covered. If you observe Advent and Lent, your Christmas and Easter are going to be God-times naturally.

Let's take a look at how these God-given opportunities for celebration work.

How Is This a God Thing?

When Jesus got together with his disciples in the upper room on the night before he died, he gave them some important instructions and showed them how to carry them out. Lifting up the bread, he gave thanks for it, broke it, and gave it to them. "This is my body given for you; do this in remembrance of me," he told them (Luke 22:19).

Then, picking up the cup of wine, he gave thanks for it and told his disciples to drink from that same cup. Then he told them, "This cup is the new covenant in my blood, which is poured out for you" (Luke 22:20).

Jesus was using the bread and wine as symbols of his body and blood, so that when he was gone, his friends would always remember that he lived on within them, strengthening them and helping them grow the way food helps our bodies to grow. He established a ritual and made that ritual holy. Whether we celebrate Holy Communion once a year or every Sunday, it is a vivid reminder that Jesus is alive, living inside each one of us.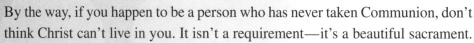
By the way, if you happen to be a person who has never taken Communion, don't think Christ can't live in you. It isn't a requirement—it's a beautiful sacrament.

What's a sacrament? It's a physical reminder—something you can see with your eyes—that helps you understand a wonderful truth you can't see.

If that's confusing, think about these examples. A wedding is a sign that two people are married. A baptism is a sign that somebody's ready to put Christ in charge of his or her life. A funeral is a sign that someone has died and we're saying good-bye.

Holidays can be signs too. They are holy days when ...

- we think about God while we are celebrating them.
- we ask God to use our celebration as he wishes.
- we remember that these celebrations were initiated by God and we are privileged to take part in them.
- our celebration leaves us with an impression, almost like a footprint, that reminds us of the importance of the thing we're celebrating. So we remember not only the Easter eggs but also Jesus rising from the dead, not only dressing up like wise men but also God showing himself to us in a real, human life we can understand.

The best thing about holy days is that they don't just last for a day at a time. The Holy Spirit uses the lessons we learn all year long. If you celebrate Christmas with all its sacred symbols and you understand what Jesus' coming here was about, you're going to have Jesus on your mind all the time, reminding you of what kind of person he grew up to be and how you can grow up to be like him. With five days and seasons to celebrate, you're bound to be filled up with God all year long!

CHECK Yourself OUT

Maybe that all makes sense to you already and you want to go for it right now. Or you may be finding all this a little unsettling, because, frankly, you have always liked the egg hunt and the present opening just the way they are, thank you very much. Or it may be that you don't care a lot about holidays one way or the other, except for the fact that you don't have to do math on those days.

Before you read on, why not check out your current holiday 'tude. Choose the answer in each set of three that completes its statement in the way that is the most true for you (even if it doesn't describe you exactly). Be honest! There's no right or wrong reason—there is only you.

The first thing I think about when Thanksgiving is over and Christmas is on its way is . . .

    a.   _____there will be presents and a Christmas tree and stuff baking in the kitchen and my favorite Christmas songs and a huge turkey dinner.

    b.   _____I probably won't get what I want, my dad will be grouchy, and all my cousins are coming, and I'll have to entertain them.

    c.   _____we'll light the Advent candles and get the manger scene out and start Mary and Joseph on their journey and practice for the pageant at church.

When I start getting ready for Easter . . .

    a.   _____I want to shop for a new outfit and dye eggs and hope I'm not too old for an Easter basket, with those wonderful chocolate bunnies.

    b.   _____I don't want to go to church because my outfit is dumb, and I don't want any candy because I'll get fat, and I don't want to hide eggs for the little kids because I know I'll step in dog poop.

    c.   _____I can't wait to sing all those Christ-has-risen songs and see everything looking all colorful and newborn.

When Halloween rolls around . . .

    a.   _____I get my costume ready, make a new trick-or-treat bag, and beg my parents to let me go to the haunted house.

    b.   _____I wonder if I'm too old to wear a costume and go out trick or treating, and I dread those parties where they make you bob for apples and get your hair all wet.

    c.   _____I kind of ignore it because I'm not into ghosts and goblins and witches and all that other stuff that doesn't seem very Christian.

Although I do kind of envy kids who are having fun with it and getting candy.

During that really long stretch between Easter and Halloween . . .

    a.   _____I get totally into Memorial Day, Fourth of July, Labor Day, and the whole beach and vacation thing.

    b.   _____I get really bored because except for summer vacation there's not that much to celebrate.

    c.   _____I wish we had more holidays that are holy days, and I'd like to know more about the ones other people celebrate—like the Feast of the Pentecost.

Count up your *a*'s, *b*'s, and *c*'s and write the numbers in the spaces below:

"*a*" _____

"*b*" _____

"*c*" _____

If you had more *a*'s, you are a person who really likes to celebrate—and that's good! You have a sense of joy and fun and excitement that jazzes up everybody around you. As you read this book, you'll want to find out how you can carry that celebration side of yourself into the sacred observance of the holy days. You won't have to give up the Easter basket or the cookie baking. You'll just learn more ways to make the holy days special, ways that will have even more meaning to you than "Let's party!" You're going to have a good time with this book.

If you had more *b*'s, your zest for holidays has kind of fizzled out. Maybe you've had a lot of disappointments, or as you've gotten older the kid side of the celebrations has stopped being fun. This is good because it means you are dissatisfied with the way you have celebrated these days in the past, and you're ready for a change. As you read this book, look for ideas that inspire you—that make you want to get up and try them out. Then go for it. You may end up with a brand-new holiday 'tude.

If you had more ❀'s, you probably already see how precious these holy days can be and how they are one of the ways you can feel God close to you. As you read this book, you'll get all kinds of new ideas for making your celebrations even more sacred. Don't forget to share them with friends who may fall into the "b" category!

Girlz WANT TO KNOW

❀ *LILY: I'm already jazzed about celebrating holy days, and I haven't even read the book yet! But I also already know that if I suggest anything to my family, my brothers are going to say I'm freaking out and my mom's going to say, "I don't think we have the time or the money for all that stuff, Lily." I'm afraid I'm never gonna be able to make any of it happen.*

Lil, you have the challenge a lot of go-get-'em, high-energy girls have. You go after everything 150 percent and don't understand why it wears your family out! That isn't a bad thing—a world without Lilys would be a pretty boring place. But it does mean you'll need to adjust your enthusiasm to the rest of the household. Try this.

- Make a super-duper wish list of everything you'd like to do in observing a holiday in a sacred way (as you read further in this book).
- Go through your list and cross out anything you already know isn't going to get parental approval—like acting out the manger scene on the front lawn every night for the whole twelve days of Christmas, using live animals, your dad in a Joseph costume, well, you get the idea.

- Put a star by the remaining ideas that you *really* want to do.
- Then go to your folks with this simplified, streamlined plan. If it still isn't streamlined enough for them, negotiate for a few of the ideas with the stars by them.
- If you have to be content with only one of your new additions to the family celebration, let that be enough for now and make it wonderful. Next time, your parents might be open to a few more of your suggestions.
- Remember that your siblings may not get what the big deal is all about and that could cause them to pooh-pooh just about anything you come up with. So don't expect rave reviews and undying gratitude even if it does come off well. Unless, of course, you ask them to contribute some suggestions of their own.

❀ *SUZY: This all sounds wonderful, but my problem is that my family doesn't even go to church. I go with my friends. If I come home and start talking about Jesus while we're dyeing Easter eggs—well, I'm not sure how that's going to go over.*

That's a toughie—not just when it comes to holidays but the rest of the time as well. Maybe suggestions about making holidays more sacred will give you a chance to show them how going to church and developing a relationship with God is making a difference to you. Maybe they would be more open to your explaining the Jesse Tree you're making for your room than if you suddenly started chattering at the dinner table about Isaiah's prophecies. Just keep a couple of things in mind:

- Start small, maybe with something that involves only you. Then add things that include them a little at a time—maybe even when next Easter or Epiphany comes around.
- Don't try to shove it down anybody's throat or make your family feel like they're "less than" because they don't go to church Christmas Eve or don't know what the word *Pentecost* means. The last thing you want to do is let anybody think Christianity is some kind of exclusive society

they can get into only if they're good enough or if they observe certain holy days. Make what you do inviting and nonthreatening.

- Don't push, whine, plead, beg, or do anything that is sure to get you sent to your room. If your family isn't ready, back off, pray for them, and observe the holy days the best you can. God won't let you be lonely in it for long. Hang in there.

❀ *RENI: I'm confused. I have some friends who say that if you don't take Communion every Sunday or you miss church on Good Friday, you aren't saved unless you do all this repenting—I don't know. It makes it sound like you have to celebrate these holy days or God won't love you or something.*

It sounds like your friends are the ones who are a little confused. Let's see if we can't set things straight for you. Sacraments—like Communion and baptism—and the sacred celebration of holy days are reminders of the things they represent. You take Communion to remind you that Jesus gave his body and blood so that you can live with him alive in you. It isn't the bread or the wine or the grape juice that are important. And it isn't how often you take them that's the real deal either. It's what you remember and how you practice those things in your life that matters to God.

If you were stranded on an island and you never took Communion, you could still be in relationship with the Lord. But as long as you're not living on an island all alone, it helps to take Communion side-by-side with other people who want the same thing you do. So you don't have to celebrate the holy days, but you do need to make Jesus your friend and promise him you will always follow his way for you. You also need to study the Bible and open yourself up to the Holy Spirit by praying and being part of a community of believers. The holy days can refresh you as you do those things and make you want to keep going.

Just Do It

Ready to get started? Here's all you have to do for now.

Get yourself a calendar for this year—the kind with squares big enough to

write things in. If you start reading this book in the fall, try to get next year's calendar too. If you can't get your hands on store-bought calendars, you can either make one—that can be a lot of fun—or ask your parents if any businesses have given them calendars lately. (Some do that as advertising.) You'll use your calendar in the **Just Do It** section of each chapter of this book.

That's it. You're set to go! Except for one thing, of course.

Talking to God About It

Fill in the blanks on this prayer outline or talk to God in the way you've learned is best for you, including these kinds of things:

Dear _____ (your favorite way of addressing our Lord),

I'm about to learn about holy days—times when I can celebrate you in a special, sacred way. First of all, will you forgive me for the way I might have treated your holy days in the past? You know, like when I _____. I really do love it that we have days set aside just to focus on you. Please, God, help me with the things I'm checking off on this list that I need special help with when it comes to celebrating.

_____ *Sometimes I get pretty carried away with projects and drive everybody nuts.*

_____ *Sometimes it's hard for me to get motivated to do something different—like I'm afraid or too lazy!*

_____ *Sometimes I get really excited about doing something like this but then I don't follow through until I'm finished.*

_____ *I'm thinking I like my holidays just the way they are, except that they need to be more sacred, more about you.*

_____ *I'm afraid my family will think my ideas are stupid and they will laugh at me.*

Will you please be in the hearts of these people whom I think would get a lot out of celebrating holy days but might not think it's such a great idea at first:

_____

_____

Thank you, God, for all the things and people you have placed in my life that will make this easier for me.

Please know that I'm offering all of this up to you, God—that it's all about you. I want it to be_____

Before I say Amen, I'm going to close my eyes and listen for you. Please help me to hear, somehow, some way, what you want me to know. I love you, God.

The best holiday I ever had was ...

_____

_____

_____

_____

_____

_____

_____

_____

_____

_____

_____

Christmas Is Coming!

**Prepare the way for the Lord,
make straight paths for him.**
Matthew 3:3

For most of us, it can be July and if somebody mentions Christmas, we can suddenly almost smell the tree. By the time December comes along, we can hardly stand the excitement. There's so much to do—so much to look forward to.

It's all about a thing called anticipation, which is what gives you that same sizzle under your skin when you're getting ready to go on a trip or planning your birthday party or counting the days until school's out for the summer. Sometimes looking ahead to something is as much fun as doing it.

The four weeks of waiting time before Christmas is called Advent, which comes from the Latin word *adventus,* meaning "arrival." It's a time to prepare for the arrival of Jesus.

But it's not about shopping, decorating, baking, and wishing for a pile of presents under the tree. Advent is about getting yourself ready inside. That means that while you're getting everything all decked out for the celebration, you also need to take time to think about the true meaning of the celebration. During Advent, you can do that by . . .

- looking at yourself and making sure there isn't anything you're doing or thinking that could make you even a little bit funky about Jesus coming and seeing you the way you are right now.
- praying about those things and getting some help from God to change them.
- learning how having Jesus in your life can make everything better.

When you use Advent as preparation time, Christmas becomes even more of a celebration, and for all the right reasons. How do we know that? Because— of course—it's a God-thing.

How Is This a God Thing?

God started getting the world ready for Jesus centuries before he arrived. (Now, *that's* planning ahead!) When the prophet Isaiah was alive, God's people had been taken away from their Promised Land and were in exile in Babylon— which meant they couldn't go back to their homes. It would be like being chased out of your neighborhood and not being allowed to return and get your stuff or see your house.

If anybody ever needed to be reassured that things were going to get better, it was those people! So God, knowing the people would be discouraged in captivity, had instructed Isaiah to write down words of comfort, telling them that help was on the way—even before the captivity took place. He was going to send a Messiah, a Savior, who was going to make life good for them again. You've probably heard what Isaiah said to them: "The people walking in darkness have seen a great light. . . . For to us a child is born, to us a son is given. . . . And he will be called Wonderful Counselor, Mighty God, Everlasting Father, Prince of Peace" (Isaiah 9:2, 6). That pretty much covered everything they would ever need.

From then on, God's people lived in eager anticipation of this Wonderful Counselor who was going to come and show them how to live a God-like life. So when, centuries later, John the Baptist showed up—a man with a strange wardrobe and diet—and told the people that the Messiah was coming very soon, the anticipation mounted.

John preached, "'Repent, for the kingdom of heaven is near.' This is he who was spoken of through the prophet Isaiah: A voice of one calling in the desert, 'Prepare the way for the Lord, make straight paths for him'" (Matthew 3:2–3).

A lot of people were impressed by John the Baptist and thought he was the Messiah, but he set them straight on that right away. He said all he could do was prepare them for the real Savior. He told them they should prepare themselves by . . .

- repenting—being truly sorry for the rotten things they were doing and turning their lives around.
- not thinking that just because they were part of Abraham's family that they were automatically going to be saved by this Savior.
- making room in their cluttered minds for the new message the Messiah was going to bring them. (See Matthew 3:2–10.)

By the time John started spreading that word, Jesus was already a grown man. But before he was born, God sent an angel to prepare the young woman who was going to give birth to him. She had to know that this was going to be no ordinary baby but the Son of God himself. That wasn't something he wanted to spring on Mary without giving her any time to get herself ready for that awesome responsibility. You can read her incredible story in Luke 1:26–38.

It's just as important for us to prepare for the arrival of Jesus as it was for the exiles in Babylon and for Mary and for the people John the Baptist preached to. Every year, Advent gives us time to focus on Jesus coming into our lives and becoming more and more a part of us. If you observe Advent in a sacred way that makes a deep impression in your mind, you'll find yourself focusing on you and Jesus throughout the year. Let's find out how.

CHECK Yourself OUT

We'll start by finding out what the preparation for Christmas is like in your house. Remember, we're not trying to find out if your family is sacred enough! It's a good idea to know where you are now so you'll know where to start in making the holy days of Advent more meaningful.

Circle the letter of the words in each set that best describe you and your family (even if they aren't an exact description).

The feeling in my house in December is usually . . .

a. _____ hectic and tense.

b. _____ busy and excited.

c. _____ peaceful and hopeful.

The thing my family focuses on the most just before Christmas is . . .

a. _____ getting everything done.

b. _____ making the preparations fun.

c. _____ being sure all the preparations are about Jesus' birthday.

By the time Christmas Day finally arrives, my parents are . . .

a. _____ glad it's over.

b. _____kind of letdown and bummed out after all the excitement of getting ready.

c. _____ready to celebrate the great day!

Christmas Eve or Christmas Day is a time when we go to church . . .

a. _____almost never.

b. _____one of the few times all year.

c. _____always, like we do on Sundays.

If I could change anything about the way my family gets ready for Christmas, I would want it to be . . .

a. _____happier and not so stressful.

b. _____less busy and more sacred but still as happy as it is now.

c. _____just the same because it's happy *and* sacred.

Count up the number of *a*'s, *b*'s, and *c*'s you circled. Put the numbers in the right slots:

"*a*" _____

"*b*" _____

"*c*" _____

Remember as you read about your score that this is just a way to see where you are and how to use this book in the best way possible for you. Read all the score explanations because, who knows, your family may fit into all three in some way.

If you circled more *a*'s, Christmas might be a pretty stressful time around your house. Maybe your family tries to do it all and everybody gets so tired it's hard to enjoy any of it. Or maybe your mom and/or dad feel really pressured to make everything wonderful every minute for all of you, which is impossible. And then they get pretty cranky as a result. Or maybe because of the focus on gifts, Christmas brings out everybody's greedy, jealous side—not anyone's best side. If that's the case, this chapter can probably help you a lot. Read carefully and see if you're inspired to suggest a few changes next Christmas or even make a few for yourself. It could keep you from being nervous and disappointed when December rolls around again.

If you circled more ♭'s, preparation for Christmas at your house is probably busy and fun and exciting, but the presents and decorations and parties may be getting a lot more attention than Jesus. That might have occurred to you, or maybe you're just now thinking about it. This chapter is worth reading for you, because you may find some ways to make your family's Christmas sacred *and* fun. Even if nobody else in your family is interested in including more about the birth of Jesus amid all the other stuff that's already going on, you can use some of the ideas you find in this book to make your private preparation sacred.

If you circled more ℭ's, your family has probably already discovered how to keep Jesus as the whole reason for celebrating, and it has made your Christmas season less nervous and more enjoyable. There's a chance you will already know about some of the ideas described in this chapter, but read on. We all need a little inspiration—and maybe some new material—now and then.

Girlz WANT TO KNOW

❀ *LILY: Do I have to give up everything about Christmas that's not sacred? I kind of like watching* **The Miracle on Thirty-fourth Street** *and making gingerbread men.*

You definitely don't have to give up all the secular traditions in order to keep Christ in your Christmas. The idea is (1) not to let them take over so the manger scene gets stuck behind the Christmas tree and you kind of forget about Jesus, and (2) to make everything you do in your celebration a God-thing.

You can say a special prayer while you're decorating the tree—either to yourself or with your family if they're open to it—thanking God for being as full of life as the evergreen. You can give each gift as a gift to Jesus, because any time you are generous to someone, you're being generous to him. That's in Matthew 10:42, if you want to read about it.

If there's anything about your preparation for Christmas or your celebration of it that you can't see as a God-thing, that would be a tradition worth giving up. This would be stuff like giving your brother a gag gift that hurts his feelings, putting everything you can think of on your wish list, or checking out your brothers' or sisters' present piles to make sure they aren't bigger than yours.

✿ *RENI: So what's the deal with Santa Claus? Some Christians say it's okay to include Santa in your Christmas, and others say it's right up there with worshiping idols. Which is right?*

That's a tough question. Maybe a little about the history of the old guy will help your family make a decision.

In the fourth century—we're talking seventeen hundred years ago—a man named St. Nicholas lived in what is now southern Turkey. He was a bishop and is considered to be the special saint of children. In those days, when a man wanted a husband for his daughter, he had to be able to provide her with a dowry, which was money and goods to help the couple get started.

The legend goes that in the community where St. Nicholas lived, there was a man so poor he couldn't get a dowry together for any of his three daughters. St. Nicholas secretly gave all three of them dowries so they would not be shamed. His gift was supposedly given on the sixth day of December. That's where the tradition of giving gifts on Christmas began.

People liked the story and the tradition so much that it spread, eventually reaching Holland, where in the Dutch language St. Nicholas is translated as Sinter Klaas. The Dutch people pictured him as a bishop who arrived by ship and rode a large white horse that could gallop over the rooftops as well as on land.

When the Puritans left England to settle in the New World (what is now America), they lived for a time in Holland, and later the Dutch people established a colony in the New World. When December came around, the legend of Sinter Klaas naturally came up, and the name somehow came out as Santa Claus. People envisioned him in different ways, but when a man named Clement Moore wrote a poem for his kids in 1822, describing St. Nick, he said he was a "jolly old elf" who rode around in a "miniature sleigh with eight tiny reindeer."

That poem is *The Night Before Christmas* and was published in a newspaper and became so famous that just about everybody in the United States began to think about Santa Claus the way Clement Moore had described him, complete with a huge belly and a red suit, coming to deliver gifts to kids on the night of December 24.

As you can see, the idea of Santa Claus isn't bad or even un-Christian. The problem is that little kids often love Santa more than they do Jesus. After all, they can sit on his lap (or the lap of a pretty good imitation!) and pour out a list of their hearts' desires. If you have little kids in your family, your parents will want to consider how important Santa is in your house, and maybe you can help with that. If your younger brothers and sisters think Christmas is a celebration of Santa's birthday, you might want to tone down the St. Nick thing and get Jesus in clearer view!

✿ *ZOOEY: Did you know they won't even let us talk about Christmas at school? We're supposed to call it "the holiday season," and in music class, we can only sing stuff like "Jingle Bells" and that one about the chestnuts. We can't do "Silent Night" or "Away in a Manger" or anything that has to do with God or Jesus. What's up with that?*

Christmas is sometimes the first clue Christian kids get that there's a big conflict in our schools about separating church and state. You'll notice that you don't pray in school as a class and that teachers don't discuss their beliefs with their students. That all stems from what the authors of the Bill of Rights wrote, that everyone should have the freedom to worship however they want to or not worship at all, if that's what they choose.

Some people feel that since you're a captive audience in school and can't get up and walk out of a classroom if the talk turns to God and you don't believe in God, *any* talk about religious things is violating a person's religious freedom. Some people are so sensitive about it that they spend a lot of time looking for violations that might make somebody uncomfortable but that nobody else thinks twice about.

It can be very hard on you as a Christian. The more your life centers around your faith, the more you want to express that in what you do. And you should know that many people feel that our founding fathers would be disheartened to find that we have left God out of our public schools. But unless you go to a Christian school, you'll run into this difficulty. That's why it's so important to make your preparation and celebration at home as sacred as you can.

Just Do It

Before you start on any of these ideas, keep these things in mind:

- You don't have to do all of them. The idea is to make the season more meaningful, not more crowded. Choose one or maybe two, and let it be rich and delicious. Then maybe next year you can add one or two more. Include your family if they're willing and interested, but don't try to force anything on anyone. (You know, like pitching a fit and saying, "Why doesn't anybody ever want to do what I want to do?")

- Most of these traditions can be enjoyed by yourself or with your friends if your family isn't up for them right now. You can even pass them on to your Sunday school teacher. He or she might be delighted to try them in class.

- Don't nag your parents for money to buy supplies, especially in December, when they will already have a lot of extra expenses. (Where do you think all those presents come from?) If you don't have enough allowance or babysitting money, try to make do with what's around the house. Sometimes the more creative you have to be, the more the project will mean to you later.

- Don't worry about being artistic enough to pull off some of these things. What's important is that whatever you do helps you remember how generous God was to send his Son here to show us how much he loves us and to save us from our sin.

Take out your calendar and find Christmas (that's December 25, in case it slipped your mind). Find the Sunday before Christmas and write FOURTH SUNDAY IN ADVENT in that square. (If Christmas falls on a Sunday, the Sunday before that is the fourth Sunday in Advent, which would be December 18.) Now work backward and fill in the THIRD SUNDAY IN ADVENT, the SECOND SUNDAY IN ADVENT, and the FIRST SUNDAY IN ADVENT.

Now you can see the whole season of Advent. Of course, we're always supposed to be making more and more room inside for Jesus, but the season of Advent gives you a chance to concentrate on it. By the way, in Christian churches where Advent is observed, the color used for it is purple or blue, so you might want to use a purple or blue marker to label your calendar—but it isn't required.

Advent Wreath

What Is It? This is a wreath you set on a table. It's covered with greens and has four candles in it, three purple and one pink. (We'll explain why below.)

How Is It Used? On the first Sunday in Advent, one purple candle should be lit. This can be done at dinnertime, during family devotions if your family has them, or during your quiet time. If you're doing this by yourself, you'll need to get permission first. Below we'll give some suggestions for things to do and think about when you light the candle. Light the same candle every day at the same time for the first week.

On the second Sunday in Advent, you'll light the first candle and a second purple one and continue to do that for the second week. On the third Sunday, you'll add the pink candle, and on the fourth, you'll add the final purple candle.

What Does It Mean?

- The greens signify the ever-living love of God.
- The purple is a traditional color for royalty, and it's used to celebrate Christ's coming as King.

- The pink represents joy, and you use it on the third candle because that's the week you'll be focusing on joy (which we'll talk about shortly).
- The circular shape of the wreath symbolizes God, who has no beginning and no end but continues on forever.
- The lighting of the candles, adding one a week, shows us the light Jesus brings getting brighter and brighter as he gets closer and closer. It's like stepping into the sun to get warm or watching plants turn greener and fresher when you put them closer to the light. Most of us feel a lot more cheerful on sunny days. You get the idea. "The people walking in darkness have seen a great light; on those living in the land of the shadow of death a light has dawned" (Isaiah 9:2). So the light Jesus sheds on our lives lets us clearly see where we're going and which direction we need to take. It also lets us see the healing, the love, the joy, and the peace we find when we focus on God.

How Can You Make It? There are a lot of different ways you can put together an Advent wreath. How you make yours depends on whether it's going to be a family project or a solo effort and whether you're going to go out and buy all new supplies or go with what you have around the house. The important thing is to do it thinking about how real it's going to make the importance of Jesus' coming in your life. Here are a few suggestions—or you can come up with your own:

- Kits are available in stationery, arts and crafts, and Christian supply stores.
- You can buy a Styrofoam ring (green if you can find one), three purple candles and one pink one, and florist's pins. Then you can gather greens from your yard (with permission) or buy artificial ones. Then do this:
  - Poke four holes for your candles in the Styrofoam, using the candles.

- Attach greens to the Styrofoam with the florist's pins. Be as creative as you want because there is no right or wrong way to arrange them.
  - Put your candles in, and you're ready to go.
  - Or you can put four candleholders on the table, put the candles in them, and make a circle around them with greens. It doesn't even have to be a perfectly round arrangement. It's the thought and prayer you put into it that counts.

What If

- I don't have any greens? Put an artificial wreath on the table and put four candles in holders at its edges.
- The candles I have aren't purple or pink? Use some other color and think purple and pink!
- I don't have candleholders? Put some play dough in four disposable paper cups and stick a candle in each one.
- My mom won't let me light candles? Make fake flames out of aluminum foil.

Jesse Tree

What Is It? A tree or a picture of a tree that is decorated more and more as Christmas approaches.

How Is It Used? Starting on December 1, a new ornament is added each day (we'll explain below) to symbolize a characteristic of God's love—which is so huge, we need at least twenty-five different ways to think of it!

What Does It Mean? As far back as Jesse—who was King David's father—God was planning the birth of his son into our world to show us how to live and to die on the cross to save us from our sins. "A shoot will come up from the stump of Jesse; from his roots a Branch will bear fruit" (Isaiah 11:1).

As you add symbols, you get a better and better feel for how rich God is—how he has everything covered.

How Can You Make It? Try one of these.

The tree:

- You can use a live or artificial miniature Christmas tree—or any kind of bush, as long as the gardener in your house says it's okay.
- You can take one evergreen bough (maybe one of the ones that gets cut off your Christmas tree if you get it up early enough) and put it in a pot, bucket, or big coffee can, using dirt, sand, gravel, or even marbles to hold it up.
- You can draw or paint a Christmas tree (minus the ornaments) on poster board or a big piece of paper and put it on your wall.

The ornaments:

- Draw the ornaments on index cards or construction paper, color them, and cut them out. If you are using a tree, put a hole in the top of each ornament and tie a loop of string or ribbon through it for hanging. If you're using a drawing of a tree, hang the ornaments with tape.
- Cut the ornaments out of fabric and glue trims or sequins on them. See above for how to hang them.
- Cut circles out of paper and draw the symbols on them. See above for how to hang them.

The symbols you'll need:

Dec. 1	dove	Dec. 9	bowl	Dec. 17	stalk of grain
Dec. 2	apple	Dec. 10	stone tablets	Dec. 18	big fish
Dec. 3	rainbow	Dec. 11	horn	Dec. 19	watchtower
Dec. 4	small star	Dec. 12	water jar	Dec. 20	sun
Dec. 5	ram	Dec. 13	lyre	Dec. 21	scallop shell
Dec. 6	ladder	Dec. 14	altar	Dec. 24	big star
Dec. 7	grain sack	Dec. 15	piece of coal		
Dec. 8	burning bush	Dec. 16	king's crown		

Advent Calendar

What Is it? A special kind of calendar with a small door or flap, which is opened each day to reveal something that draws us closer to Jesus' coming. An Advent calendar you buy might have a piece of chocolate for each day or a picture that makes you think about preparing for Christmas. The calendar we're suggesting will have a small task you can do for someone else or sometimes for yourself.

How Is It Used? Each day, beginning December 1 (just to keep it simple, even though Advent usually begins in late November), you'll open a new door or flap and do what is stated there. It's one way to make room inside yourself for Jesus.

What Does It Mean? Waiting for anything that's going to be really wonderful—like Christmas—can be difficult. Time seems to go into slow motion, just when you want it to pick up speed, and you can't understand why your parents say things like, "I can't believe it's only two weeks until Christmas." *Only?* you think. *Two weeks is an eternity!*

The trick in Advent is to make the waiting mean something. If you do some small thing each day to help someone else or do something that is going to make you an ounce better than you are, the days will go by faster and each one will bring you closer, not just to Christmas but to Christ himself.

How Can You Make It?

The calendar:

- You can use a calendar you already have—even the one you're using for all your holy days, as long as it has squares big enough to write in—and the bigger the better.
- You can make a December calendar on poster board or a big piece of paper to hang on the wall.

The flaps:

- Any kind of paper will do as long as you can't see through it.
- Cut one square for each day in December, the same size as the squares on your calendar with a little bit extra.
- Fold down that extra part and glue or tape only that to the square, so you can lift it like a flap.

What goes under each flap:

- On a piece of binder paper, make a list of all the important people in your life. Think about family members, friends, teachers, people at your church, neighbors, relatives—everybody who makes your life a little different than it would be if that person weren't in it.
- Next to each name, write some small thing you could do for that person that would make him or her smile, laugh, or feel good or that would relieve a little bit of that person's workload. For example, could you do the dishes for your sister one night, play a game of "Go Fish" with your little brother, make a card for the lady who takes you and the other kids across the street at the crosswalk every day? Be creative. If you can't think of something to do for someone, ask that person, "What little chore could I do for you that would make you happy or save you some time?"
- If you don't have twenty-five names and tasks—and most people won't— write your name on the rest of the lines. Next to your name on each line, write down something you could do that would make you a better person. Here are some suggestions to check off:
  ❏ Don't tease my brother for a whole day.
  ❏ Tell everybody in my family I love them at least once.

❏ Tell somebody I'm sorry for something I did.

❏ Pick out a Bible verse that seems to be written to or about *me* and memorize it.

❏ Don't fight over the TV remote or the front seat or the last cookie.

❏ Being sure you have twenty-five tasks, write one in each square of your Advent calendar and close the flap.

• Hang your calendar or prop it up where you can see it. You're ready for December 1.

The Weeks of Advent

Let's look at how that all fits together when Advent begins. Remember that you don't have to do all of these things. If you're doing one or two, you can skip over the ones that don't apply to you.

Advent begins on a different date every year. So we've given you a schedule starting with December 1. If the first Sunday in Advent is before December 1, start using your Advent wreath on that date and begin the other activities on December 1.

December 1: Light the first candle on your Advent wreath. Read Genesis 1:1 through Genesis 2:3 or read the story of creation in a Bible storybook. Hang the dove on your Jesse tree—the symbol of God's Spirit moving over the waters at the beginning. All day, take special note of all the wonderful things God has created for us because he loves us. And then complete the task listed on your Advent calendar.

December 2: Light the appropriate candle(s) on your Advent wreath. Read Genesis 2:4 through Genesis 3:13, or read the story of Adam and Eve in a Bible storybook. Hang the apple on your Jesse tree—the symbol of the need to obey God. Think today about how well you obey God, your parents, and your teachers and about how you could do an even better job of that. Complete the task on your Advent calendar.

December 3: Light the appropriate candle(s) on your Advent wreath. Read Genesis 6:11–22, Genesis 7:17 through Genesis 8:3, and Genesis 9:8–17, or read the story of Noah and the flood in a Bible storybook. Hang the rainbow on your Jesse tree—the sign of God's promise never again to destroy the world with a flood. Think today about the promises God has kept to you and how good you are at keeping the promises you make. Complete the task on your Advent calendar.

December 4: Light the appropriate candle(s) on your Advent wreath. Read Genesis 12:1–7 and Genesis 15:1–6, or read the story about Abram in a Bible storybook. Hang the small star on your Jesse tree—the symbol of God's promise to Abram that his ancestors would be as many people as there are stars in the sky. It's also the symbol of God's plan for each of our lives. Think today about what God's plan might be for you and how much you are (or aren't!) paying attention to what that might be. Complete the task on your Advent calendar.

December 5: Light the appropriate candle(s) on your Advent wreath. Read Genesis 22:1–19, or read the story of Abraham and Isaac in a Bible storybook. Hang the ram on your Jesse tree—the symbol that God wants our obedience more than our sacrifice. Think today about what you could give up that would make you more obedient to God and give that up for today—like watching TV, getting your own way, or hogging the computer. Complete the task on your Advent calendar.

December 6: Light the appropriate candle(s) on your Advent wreath. Read Genesis 28:1–17, or read the story of Jacob and the ladder in a Bible storybook.

Hang the ladder on the Jesse tree—the symbol that God always goes with us, no matter where we go. Think today about God being with you when you're doing hard things, like taking a test or admitting you made a mistake. Complete the task on your Advent calendar.

December 7: Light the appropriate candle(s) on your Advent wreath. (Depending on what date Advent started, you may have added the second candle by now.) Read Genesis 42:1 through Genesis 45:15, or read about Joseph and his brothers in a Bible storybook. Hang the sack of grain on your Jesse tree—the symbol of forgiveness and reconciliation (making up or getting things settled once and for all). Today think about somebody you need to make up with or forgive or be forgiven by and see if you can't get that taken care of. Complete the task for today on your Advent calendar.

December 8: Light the appropriate candle(s) on your Advent wreath. Read Exodus 1:1–14 and Exodus 3:1–12, or read the story of Moses and the burning bush in a Bible storybook. Hang the burning bush on the Jesse tree—the symbol of being chosen by God to do a particular thing. Today think about what God seems to have chosen you to do right now—things like helping with the younger kids in your family, tutoring other kids in your class, improving your grades so you'll be ready for whatever God has for you in the future. Complete the task on your Advent calendar.

December 9: Light the appropriate candles on your Advent wreath. Read Exodus 12:1–39, or read about the Passover and escape from Egypt in a Bible storybook. Hang the bowl on the Jesse tree—the symbol of getting up and doing what God wants you to do right now, without delay. Today, think about what might be urgent in your life, something that maybe you've been putting off and you really need to do. Determine to do that today or at least get a start on it. Complete the task on your Advent calendar.

December 10: Light the appropriate candles on your Advent wreath. Read Exodus 19:16 through Exodus 20:20. Hang the tablets on the Jesse tree—the symbol of God's laws and their importance in our lives. Today, decide which of the commandments you have the most trouble obeying, and work on that. Complete the task you've assigned yourself on your Advent calendar.

December 11: Light the appropriate candles on your Advent wreath. Read Joshua 1:1–9 and Joshua 5:13 through Joshua 6:20, or read about the battle of Jericho in a Bible storybook. Hang the horn on the Jesse tree—the symbol of God being in charge no matter who the earthly leader may be. Today think about whom God has put in charge of your life while you're a kid and honor that person or those people with at least a thank you. Complete the task on your Advent calendar.

December 12: Light the appropriate candles on your Advent wreath. Read Judges 2:6–16, Judges 6:1–16, and Judges 7:1–23, or read about Gideon in a Bible storybook. Hang the water jar on the Jesse tree—the symbol for God always raising up someone to get people out of the trouble even when they have brought it on themselves. Today think about any trouble you may have brought on yourself, maybe by lying or trying to escape being punished or being unkind to a friend. Go to a grown-up who can help you with that. Also, complete your task on your Advent calendar.

December 13: Light the appropriate candles on your Advent wreath. Read 1 Samuel 16, 2 Samuel 5:1–5, and 2 Samuel 7:1–17, or read the story of David in a Bible storybook. Hang the little harp (lyre) on your Jesse tree—the symbol of the musician king whom God didn't give up on, in spite of all his mistakes. Today think of one mistake you've made recently, and know that if you're truly sorry and trying hard not to make that mistake again, God will forgive you and is already making you a better person inside. Go to someone and confess that sin if you need to. Then complete the assigned task on your Advent calendar.

December 14: Light the appropriate candles on your Advent wreath. Read 1 Kings 18:17–39, or read the story of Elijah in a Bible storybook. Hang the altar on your Jesse tree—the symbol that God wants to turn our hearts back to him when we start worshiping other things. Today, think about what might have become more important to you than God—that might be clothes, popularity, your Christmas wish list—and work on changing that by putting God back in his rightful place. Complete the task on your Advent calendar.

December 15: Light the appropriate candles on your Advent wreath. (If you're on the third week now, be sure the third candle you light is the pink one for joy.) Read Isaiah 6:1–13, or read about Isaiah in the temple in a Bible storybook. Hang the coal on the Jesse tree—the symbol of Isaiah's mouth being cleansed, just as ours should be. Today be very careful not to dishonor God with anything you say. Complete the job on your Advent calendar.

December 16: Light the appropriate candles on your Advent wreath. Read Isaiah 8:11 through Isaiah 9:7, or ask your mom or dad to read it and explain it to you. Hang the king's crown on the Jesse tree—the symbol of the justice and peace God promised to bring to his people. Today think of something in your life that seems unfair and messed up. Go to somebody in authority (your mom, your teacher, your pastor) and ask for that person's help in straightening it out—even if it's something very small. Complete the job on your Advent calendar.

December 17: Light the appropriate candles on your Advent wreath. Read 2 Chronicles 36:11–21 and Jeremiah 30:23 through Jeremiah 31:14, or read about Jeremiah and the Babylonian exile in a Bible storybook, or ask your mom or dad to explain it to you. Hang the stalk of grain on the Jesse tree—the symbol of promised abundance. Think about all the blessings you have in your life and thank God for them. Complete the job on your Advent calendar.

December 18: Light the appropriate candles on your Advent wreath. Read Jonah 1:1 through Jonah 4:11, or read about Jonah in a Bible storybook. Hang the big fish on your Jesse tree—the symbol that God's more interested in

having people change their ways than he is about punishing them. Think about something you've been punished for and decide whether you've changed because of it. If not, see what you can do about that today. Complete the job on your Advent calendar.

December 19: Light the appropriate candles on your Advent wreath (and don't forget to add the fourth one on the fourth Sunday in Advent, whenever that falls). Read Habakkuk 1:1–4 and Habakkuk 2:1–4, or have your mom or dad read it and explain it to you. Hang the watchtower on your Jesse tree—the symbol that if you wait and watch for God, he will act. Today think about something you're impatient about, something you want that is taking forever to happen. Ask God to help you wait, and watch for him to act on it. Complete the job on your Advent calendar.

December 20: Light the appropriate candles on your Advent wreath. Read Malachi 3:1–5 and Malachi 4:1–6, or have a grown-up read it and explain it to you. Hang the sun on your Jesse tree—the symbol that God will send the Sun of Righteousness (Jesus), who will turn people's hearts to what they should be so he won't have to destroy them. Spend some time today sitting in a sunny spot and feel the warmth. Know that it's God's healing warmth. You can be healed in your spirit—you can be better than you are because Jesus is coming to show you how. Complete the task on your Advent calendar.

December 21: Light the appropriate candles on your Advent wreath. Read Luke 1:5-17 or Matthew 3:1–6, or read about John the Baptist in a Bible storybook. Hang the scallop shell—the traditional symbol for baptism—on your Jesse tree. Today think about what your life would be like if God hadn't sent Jesus: what things would be different; how would you be different? Complete the job on your Advent calendar.

December 22: Light the appropriate candles on your Advent wreath. Read Luke 1:26–38, or read about Mary's visit from the angel in a Bible storybook. Hang the lily, the symbol of purity, on your Jesse tree. Pick one thing you do or think or say that keeps you from being pure in God's eyes and try not to do, think, or say that today. If you slip, ask God to forgive you and help you try again. Complete the job on your Advent calendar.

December 23: Light the appropriate candles on your Advent wreath. Read Matthew 1:18–25, or read about the angel's visit to Joseph in a Bible storybook. Hang on your Jesse tree the carpenter's square—the symbol for Joseph's trade and the uprightness of his life. Today, think about what you'd like to be when you grow up and decide if that would be an upright career for you—one that will allow you to serve God. Complete the task on your Advent calendar.

December 24: Light the appropriate candles on your Advent wreath. Read Luke 2:1–5, or read about Mary and Joseph's journey to Bethlehem. Hang the scroll on the Jesse tree—the symbol for Caesar's proclamation that everyone must travel to his or her place of birth to be taxed. That made the prophecy come true that the Messiah would be born in Bethlehem. Think about a coincidence that has happened in your life. Was it a coincidence, or was it God working in your life? Complete the job on your Advent calendar.

December 25: Light the appropriate candles on your Advent wreath and put one more in the center of your wreath as a Christ candle to show that the true Light of the World has steadily grown closer and is now here. Read Luke 2:6–21, or read about the birth of Jesus in a Bible storybook. Hang the big star on the top of the Jesse tree—the symbol of the star that shone down on the Christ child, just as God's love is always shining on us. From now on, God will be standing beside us to put right the things that go wrong and to bring us back to his path when we get off. Today celebrate Christmas Day with all the joy you can gather up in yourself. You're ready, because you and God have done the work together. Alleluia!

Christmas

Your family and your church, if you go to one, probably have lots of sacred traditions for Christmas already. But in case you don't feel that your Christmas celebration centers enough on Jesus' birth, here are some ideas for you. They're based on the fact that Christmas is not just a day—it's a whole season, twelve days long. Since you've probably already celebrated Christmas Day, we've provided the following suggestions.

❋❋❋ Take a homemade gift to somebody who didn't seem to receive much on Christmas Day.

❋❋❋ Tell about or draw what you would give each member of your family if you could afford anything at all for each one.

❋❋❋ Tell about or draw the gift you most want each member of your family to have two years from now.

❋❋❋ Tell about or draw the gift each member of your family gives most often to you, without even knowing it.

❋❋❋ Ask your family to help you make a list (or make one yourself if you're the only one who's up for it) of the nonmaterial things your family would like to have—like less arguing, more cooperation, more fun times together, more time with Dad.

❋❋❋ Serve your parents breakfast in bed for making your Christmas so wonderful. (If you're not a cook, keep it simple—cereal and bananas!)

❋❋❋ Write amazing thank-you notes to everyone who gave you a gift, including your parents. Go all out—glitter, paints, whatever you can find (and are allowed to use) to make sure your notes express your gratitude.

❋❋❋ Fix hors d'oeuvres before supper—even just cheese and crackers attractively arranged—and sit down with your parents. Ask them what kind of day *they* had—and listen!

❋❋❋ Bake some more Christmas goodies, since yours will be running out by now. It's still Christmas, after all!

❋❋❋ Go out and look at the stars, imagining the wise men following them to the place where the Christ child was. (You'll find out in the next chapter why now is a good time to do that.)

❋❋❋ Keep one small Christmas decoration out when everything else gets packed away (one ornament or figurine), and keep it in a place in your room where you'll see it often. It will act as a reminder that the message of Christmas should be in your life all the time.

Talking to God About It

This all seems like a lot on top of the other Christmas preparations you're sure to be making, so as you pray about Advent, keep your prayer simple. Find a spot where the light is bright. Let it shine on you, and ask God to guide you through this Advent just as he has guided every one who has trusted him since the beginning of time. That will make everything you do—whether it's an activity listed in this book or the other things you do with your family to prepare for the Christmas celebration—truly blessed and holy. Amen!

Write about something you had to wait a long, long time for ...

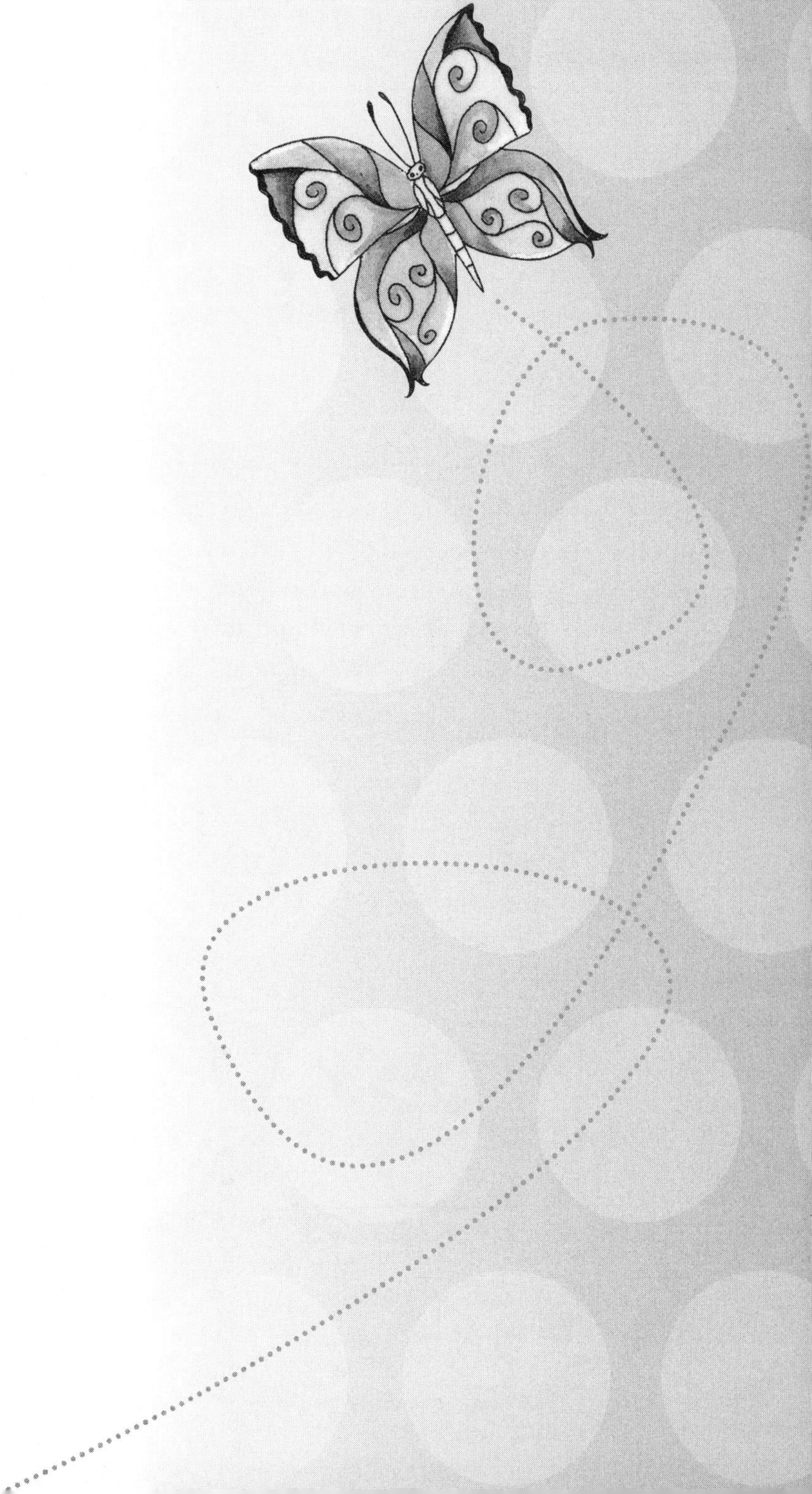

chapter 3

Making Christmas Last Longer

After Jesus was born in Bethlehem in Judea,
during the time of King Herod, Magi from
the east came to Jerusalem and asked,
"Where is the one who has been born king of the Jews?
We saw his star in the east and have come to worship him."

Matthew 2:1–2

Think back to the last Christmas pageant you were in. You probably had the two oldest kids playing Mary and Joseph, shepherds wearing bathrobes, angels hitching up those wings that never stay on—and three wise men, decked out in better bathrobes, sporting makeshift crowns, and toting jewelry boxes and fancy perfume bottles.

We're so used to thinking of the wise men—or magi—as part of the Christmas scene that it can come as a surprise to find out that they probably didn't make it to Bethlehem until much later, when Jesus was a toddler. In many Christian churches, the coming of the wise men is celebrated on January 6, in what is called the Feast of the Epiphany. It's known as Twelfth Night, for the twelfth day of the Christmas season.

Why is it called Epiphany? The name comes from the Greek word *epiphaneia*, which means the appearance of something that up until now has been invisible, such as a divine being. A divine being had definitely appeared when Jesus was born, and the wise men from the east knew it. It seems pretty obvious why that's a big deal, but there's more.

How Is This a God Thing?

Epiphany is celebrated separately in its own special feast because it was the first time the divine being—Jesus—appeared to Gentiles, that is, people other than the Jews. After all, God had promised a Messiah for the Jews, yet this Messiah was available to everybody, even non-Jews. So naturally, we non-Jews would want to recognize that with some celebrating!

It becomes even more important when we learn later on that before he ascended into heaven, Jesus said to his disciples, "Therefore go and make disciples of all nations, baptizing them in the name of the Father and of the Son and of the Holy Spirit" (Matthew 28:19). Baptize *all* nations, he said—not just the nation of Israel.

So it doesn't make sense to tack the wise men onto the end of the pageant. Those guys deserve their own pageant—or at least a little recognition—because they were the first to follow that command: "Make disciples of *all* nations." They knew they had seen God in human form. So should we.

You've just finished your Advent preparations and your Christmas celebration. (If you haven't, imagine that you have!) Check all of the following statements that are true for you right now.

_____ I feel kind of sad and let down.

_____ I wish Christmas would go on and on.

_____ I don't like this long stretch between now and Easter.

_____ Everything seems kind of ordinary now.

_____ There's stuff to look forward to now, but I wish it was still Christmastime.

There's no score for this quiz—because chances are you've checked off at least one! That's because Christmas is what we call a mountaintop experience, and as hard as we try, we can't be on top of the world all the time. Most of the time, in fact, life can be pretty ordinary.

If you checked off even one of the above, you need Epiphany—for two reasons:

- The exciting fact that God showed himself to us through Jesus—his character, his goodness, and his love—goes on all year, every year. You need to stay jazzed about that, because it's great news.
- An ordinary time—the time that follows January 6—can be a great time to appreciate how good and peaceful and rich "normal" life can be.

If you aren't convinced, read on. Maybe you will be.

Just Do It

Take out your holy day calendar. In the square for January 6, write FEAST OF THE EPIPHANY. Then look on the calendar for a day in February or March that may already have the words ASH WEDNESDAY printed in its square. (If you don't find it, ask a grown-up to look on his or her calendar; most calendars will have it.) On the square for the day before Ash Wednesday, write END OF THE EPIPHANY SEASON. By the way, in churches that observe Epiphany, the traditional color is green, so if you want to, write your labels in green marker, pencil, or ink. But remember, it isn't required.

Here are some ideas for ways to celebrate the wise men on January 6. You don't have to do them all or do them exactly this way for your Epiphany holy day to be special. It's always the thought and the prayer that goes into your celebration that counts.

- With permission or help from an adult in your house, bake a King's Cake. Bake a basic cake, and then put three gold coins (or other gold favors) in it before you put on the frosting. The coins represent the gold, frankincense, and myrrh that the Bible tells us the wise men brought to the baby Jesus. As the folks eating the cake find each of the coins, you can explain its meaning and ask all the guests to answer a question.
- Gold is the most precious metal on earth, so it represents an appropriate gift for a king. The question to ask: What's one way Jesus is king in your life?
- Frankincense, which gives off a sweet aroma, represents the Spirit of God. The question to ask: When have you recognized the Spirit of God in your life?
- Myrrh symbolizes preserving, saving, and keeping good things. Your question: What are some things in your life that need to be saved and preserved and cherished?
- Give each person in your family something precious—the gift of yourself.
- Think about what special talents and cool abilities and wonderful personality traits you have. Write them down. Next to each one, write down a way that you could use that special part of yourself as a gift to somebody in your family. Here's some examples that might help:

Lily always has imaginative ideas, to say the least. Her gift to her brother Joe (who seems to have none!) was to help him come up with an idea for his science project.

Suzy is so neat and organized it's amazing. Her gift to her sister (who tends to be a little more, shall we say, scattered) was to organize the drawers in her dresser for her.

Kresha is so bubbly, she could cheer up a statue! Her gift to her mom is the promise of a huge hug anytime her mom needs it—no questions asked.

- Find a creative way to tell each family member that the gift of *you* is available. You can make cards, come up with coupons (Good for One Free Babysitting Session, for example), or deliver funny telegrams. Then be sure to follow through!
- Since Epiphany is about blessing everyone with the message of Jesus, bless the four corners of your home, asking God to help you share his love with all who enter your home. Here's one way to do that: Go to each of the four corners of your house and say a prayer for all who will spend time there this year.

  - Because the wise men brought frankincense, it's appropriate to use a good smell in each corner, whether you give it a squirt of perfume, leave a sachet there, or fill a bowl with potpourri.
    - Make a door card, and with permission, put it above one of the doors that leads into and out of your house. The traditional door marking reads 20 + G + M + B + (current year, such as 02, 03).
    - The initials in the middle stand for Gaspar, Melchior, and Balthasar, the names traditionally assigned to the three wise men. The 20 and the current year give the year of the blessing. (Actually, there may have been more than three wise men!)

Whenever someone asks you what the sign means, you can tell about your special ceremony and how you (and perhaps your family) are trying to share the love of God with everyone who comes to your house. If your mom would prefer that you not tack the card over the front door, perhaps you could put it above the door in your room and share it with your guests.

Throughout the Epiphany season, you can make every day holy by celebrating those things that are ordinary. That doesn't mean have a party 24/7! It does mean pay attention to all the things you take for granted and let them be special. After all, Jesus did extraordinary work, like healing the sick and raising the dead, in ordinary settings—while people were getting water from a well, catching fish, going to the temple. Observing the ordinary can help you see that God's there and working—*all* the time. Here's some things you might do:

- Write a letter to a friend or a relative you usually only see or write to at Christmas or on his or her birthday.

- Pick an ordinary Friday or Saturday night, invite a friend over to spend the night, and make it a special event—for no reason. Have her favorite snacks, give her a present you've made, put up a banner welcoming her, play her favorite music—just because.

- From magazines, pull pictures of people doing ordinary things and make a collage out of them. Keep it on display in your room for a while to remind you to pray about how thankful you are for your day-to-day life (that your mom cooks your meals and washes your clothes, that you're getting a good education, that kind of thing).

- Each day during the Epiphany season, write on your calendar (maybe in green) one ordinary thing in your life that you're thankful for. Make sure it's a different thing every day. You'll be surprised how rich your life will look by Ash Wednesday—how very un-ordinary!

Girlz WANT TO KNOW

❃ *ZOOEY: My mom is so wiped out by the time Christmas Day comes, she'd freak if I said I wanted to celebrate Epiphany too!*

If the people who call the shots in your house want to take a break from celebrating, the Epiphany season is the kind of thing you can observe on your own in a quiet way. Or you might get some of your friends to do it with you. Setting aside a day or a part of a day to make it holy doesn't always have to mean you're whooping it up. Real joy is what happens when you get good news, and when you observe any holy day, however you do it, you're showing your joy over the good news that Jesus Christ brings.

❃ *RENI: My parents say this talk about Epiphany doesn't sound very Protestant to them. Are you sure it's Christian?*

Probably the reason your parents have some doubts is because the word *Epiphany* isn't familiar in all churches—not because it isn't Christian but because it isn't part of the tradition of every church. In those churches where Epiphany is celebrated, it doesn't take the place of what all Christians believe; it is merely a way of recognizing it. You don't even have to call it Epiphany if you don't want to. Just call it a celebration of God coming to us—*all* of us.

Talking to God About It

Dear _____ *(your favorite way of addressing our Father),*

In this sort of slump time after Christmas, I now have something more to celebrate. Please help me to know and understand what this season of Epiphany means in my life. I've checked off the areas where I especially need help:

_____ *chasing away the after-Christmas blues.*

_____ *being able to talk to other people about why I'm celebrating Epiphany and not being embarrassed about it.*

_____ *getting my family involved—but not pushing too hard.*

_____ *being content to do this on my own or with friends if I have to.*

_____ *knowing what gifts of myself I can give.*

_____ *following through with my plans.*

_____ *seeing God in the ordinary things in my life.*

_____ *keeping my mind on the reason for the celebration and not just the stuff that's involved.*

    God, thank you so much for making yourself visible to us through your son. Please don't ever let me forget that, whether I'm celebrating or not.

    I love you.

If you got to visit the Christ child, what gift would you bring?

Easter's on Its Way

**At once the Spirit sent him out into the desert,
and he was in the desert forty days, being
tempted by Satan.**
Mark 1:12–13

Have you noticed that almost the minute the stores take down their Christmas decorations—at least by Valentine's Day—the stuffed bunnies and egg-dyeing kits start appearing on the shelves? They make you think it's just a bunny hop in time from candy canes to Cadbury eggs.

But think again! There is a long stretch—forty days, in fact, not counting the Sundays—between the end of the Epiphany season and Easter Day, with its baskets and egg hunts and new spring clothes. It's a time called Lent, which is as important in getting ready for Easter and all that it means as Advent is in preparing for a true Christmas.

"Lent" comes from the word *lencten,* which is Anglo-Saxon (a language nobody even speaks anymore) and means the lengthening of days in the springtime—just as the longer and longer days prepare the earth for the rebirth of all those flowers and us for rebirth too.

Lent was first named and observed in the fourth century. In those days, Easter was the traditional time to be baptized, and the Christians back then set up Lent as a period of discipline and fasting for people preparing for their baptisms. As time went on, it grew into a season designed to help Christians do things like:

- getting themselves back into the habit of practicing the spiritual disciplines they may have gotten lax about—for example, reading the Bible every day and having a special time for prayer.
- giving to the church and to people who are in need.
- tossing out anything in their lives that is separating them from God.
- fasting or at least denying themselves certain things they like, in order to focus on God.

The question some people ask about Lent is, "If it isn't mentioned in the Bible, then isn't it something people dreamed up?" Is it really a God-thing? Let's take a look.

How Is This a God Thing?

All Christians agree that God sent Jesus to live and die as one of us. His death and his coming back from the dead show us that we can have eternal life if we believe in him.

His life shows us how we are supposed to live while we're here. We're not talking about leaving home and traveling around in sandals or feeding crowds of thousands with one loaf of bread. We *are* talking about having a relationship with God the Father in the same way Jesus did.

Here's how Jesus got started. He was baptized (Mark 1:9, in case you want to check it out.), and he saw the Holy Spirit on him (Mark 1:10–11). Then he did what the Spirit led him to do—spend forty days facing up to all his temptations (Mark 1:12–13). That involved several things.

- Jesus fasted, giving up earthly pleasures so he wouldn't be distracted (Matthew 4:2–4). Think of it this way—if you're having a great discussion about God in your Sunday school class and somebody comes in with a big box of donuts, where is your attention going to go? Jesus knew that, so he fasted.
- He refused to let anything come between him and God, including putting God to some kind of test (Matthew 4:5–7). What if you said to a friend, "If you're really my friend, you'll let me copy your homework," wouldn't that come between the two of you eventually?
- He disciplined himself to worship only God, even though Satan made worshiping him look pretty attractive (Matthew 4:8–10). If you started skipping church on Sundays, how soon would it be before you were thinking that things like popularity and a bunch of new stuff were more important than God?

Jesus modeled for us what we need to do in order to be one with our God. We can't just get baptized and go on our merry way—we need to have times where we look at what we're doing as Christians and make sure we're lined up with God all the way.

As you'll see below, that doesn't mean you have to give up eating for forty days and leave home to live in the desert. We'll talk about what it does mean for you, but know for now that any good discipline you practice that brings you closer to God will get you the same results Jesus experienced. When his forty days in the wilderness were over, Jesus had some pretty wonderful things happen to him:

- The devil left him alone (Matthew 4:11).

- Angels came and attended him (Matthew 4:11). This probably meant clean clothes, a soft bed, and *food*!
- Jesus went back home filled with the Holy Spirit, ready to perform miracles and teach people and do all the other amazing things God told him he could do, including saving the world from itself. (Luke 4:14).

Again, God isn't saying that if you observe Lent, you'll be lifted up by angels, removed from temptation, and given the power to make blind people see. What he does seem to be saying is that, just like Jesus, if you work at getting rid of everything that separates you from God ...

- you'll be able to resist temptation when it appears.
- your needs will always be met.
- you will be filled with the power to do whatever God has planned for your life.

Believing in Jesus is what saves you. But living as he did lets you live to the fullest right here on earth. No, you don't have to practice Lenten disciplines to be a Christian. Lent is just one of those holy times that can help you focus on what it takes to be one.

CHECK Yourself OUT

If observing Lent as a holy time sounds like something you would like to do, your first step is to identify what might be coming between you and God. God, of course, already knows what that is. He's not the one who has to get around it, because nothing keeps him from loving you. But those of us who are human can let walls build up. Let's find out which ones you and God might need to knock down this Lent.

You will find three lists below. Go through each list and put a star next to every item that is something you do or think fairly often (like more than once a month!).

LIST 1

_____ I fight with my brothers and/or sisters.
_____ I argue with my parents.
_____ I have break-ups with my friends.

_____ I do whatever I can to get my own way.

_____ I change best friends.

_____ I talk about people behind their backs.

_____ I feel left out.

_____ I hate certain people.

_____ I do or say whatever it takes to make people like me.

_____ I find out I've hurt somebody's feelings or made them mad.

_____ I have to be reminded to do my chores.

_____ I don't do my chores.

_____ I try to get out of doing my chores any way I can.

_____ I skip doing homework.

_____ I fool around in school when I'm supposed to be working.

_____ I forget to give family members phone messages.

_____ I leave my stuff around for other people to clean up after me.

_____ I forget my lunch or my P.E. clothes.

_____ I whine about having to watch my little brothers and/or sisters.

_____ I lie to keep from getting in trouble.

_____ I have to be dragged out of bed in the morning.

_____ I skip my prayer time, Bible reading, or devotions.

_____ I put off doing my homework or school projects until the last minute.

_____ I have to be reminded to brush my teeth, take my bath, that kind of thing.

_____ I have trouble keeping secrets that are okay to keep.

_____ I say stuff I'm sorry for later.

_____ I have to be forced to practice the piano or prepare for whatever lessons I'm taking.

_____ I take snacks I'm not supposed to have when nobody's looking.

_____ I let people talk me into things I know are wrong.

_____ I fail to finish projects I start.

Now count how many stars you have in each list and write the numbers in the slots below:

LIST 1 _____   LIST 2 _____   LIST 3 _____

If you had more stars in list A than in the others, you might want to work on your relationships with the other people in your life during this Lenten season. You'll find suggestions for that in the Just Do It section, but for now, be thinking about the way you treat your parents, your brothers and sisters, your friends, and even the people you aren't so crazy about. If you aren't right with them, it's pretty hard to be right with God. Lent will be a great time for you to set things straight so you can enjoy God and other people.

If you had more stars in list B than in the others, you might want to work on your sense of responsibility during Lent this year. You'll find suggestions for that in the Just Do It section. But for right now, consider how you handle the things people trust you to do—like chores, schoolwork, being a considerate member of the family. God seems to give the most responsible people the neatest stuff to do. Lent can be a good time to get strong in that area so you don't miss out.

If you had more stars in list C than in the others, you'll want to work on the area of self-discipline. You'll find suggestions for that in the Just Do It section, but at this point, take a look at how you behave when nobody's watching and what you do (and don't do) without being told a million times. It isn't easy to focus on a God we can't see. For people without self-discipline, it's practically impossible! Lent is the perfect season for getting on track with that—and for getting everybody off your back in the process.

Girlz WANT TO KNOW

Before we go any further, let's take a look at some of the things you might have heard about Lent that don't tell the whole story.

✿ *LILY: So if you give up something, like chewing gum or chocolate, isn't that doing Lent?*

Giving up something you enjoy can be part of Lenten discipline. It's like fasting, which is what Jesus did during his forty days. Giving up dessert or movies can be a good thing if it makes space for you to think more about God and how you can move closer to him. It's an even better thing if it makes you realize how hard it is for you to do things on your own, without God's strength.

But that isn't all there is to Lent—as you're about to find out if you read further. And it's not helpful if you give up something you never cared too much about in the first place—like watching the news or doing homework. If you're going to give up something as part of your observance of Lent and your preparation for Easter, it should fall into one of these categories:

- It's something that isn't good for you (like biting your nails).
- It's something that hurts other people (like gossiping).
- It's something that isn't bad but distracts you from better things (like watching TV all afternoon).

❀ *RENI: Isn't there some rule about eating fish during Lent?*

There aren't any rules when it comes to Lent. There was a time when some churches told their members not to eat meat on Fridays during Lent, and since fish is not considered meat, it was okay to eat. That came from the symbolism of the body of Christ. Since Christ's earthly body died on a Friday, not eating of the flesh on Fridays was a way of honoring that. It's another form of fasting or self-denial that can be helpful if you're thinking that way. But if you're gagging down a fish stick and thinking, "This is stupid—why can't I have a hamburger?" it's pointless. You can do other things to remind yourself that Christ gave his body for you.

❀ *ZOOEY: It sounds like Lent is kind of a bummer time. Do I have to walk around looking all sad because I know I'm a sinner and Jesus had to die for me?*

Yikes—no! Remember in the Bible, Jesus says when you fast, don't go around looking somber and disfigured so everybody will look at you and say, "Wow—isn't she religious?" (or "Isn't she a freak?"). He says wash your face and look alive so it will be obvious only to your heavenly Father that you're fasting—or doing some form of self-denial and soul-searching (Matthew 6:16–18).

And you don't have to feel sad, either. Yes, you'll be discovering things about yourself that maybe you don't like so much, but that doesn't have to be a drag. This is your chance to change those things—and that's a happy thing!

Just Do It

As always, remember that you don't have to do all of the activities suggested here. The most important thing is to do what will bring you closer to knowing God and his son, so that you can celebrate his rising from the dead when Easter Day comes.

- Take out your holy days calendar and look for Ash Wednesday, which you found when you were marking the Epiphany season. If it isn't already labeled, find Easter and count forty-six days backward. That Wednesday is called Ash Wednesday (we'll explain shortly) and is the first day in the season of Lent. The season lasts until the day before Easter. Label the season of Lent on your calendar, and if you want to use the traditional color, write it in purple. There will be a couple of other days for you to label as we go along.

- The day before Ash Wednesday is called Shrove Tuesday. Because Lent is a season of fasting and self-denial, many people like to have one last fling before the quiet Lenten season begins—that's why the famous Mardi Gras ("Fat Tuesday") in New Orleans is held the week before Ash Wednesday. Shrove Tuesday was also originally a day for using up fat and eggs (by making pancakes), which weren't to be eaten during Lent. In fact, Christians in Greece still don't use eggs or dairy products during Lent.

Because Mardi Gras in New Orleans began as a French custom, it's traditional in America to have a pancake supper on Shrove Tuesday—because they are like French crepes. So why not suggest having pancakes for supper on Shrove Tuesday—or going out to IHOP for some flapjacks smothered in whipped cream and strawberries? Even a trip to McDonald's that morning will serve the purpose. The idea is to live it up so that your time of Lent will be a big contrast. It's amazing how it makes you really notice that you've given up bubblegum or TV to make more room for God.

- Ash Wednesday, the start of Lent, is traditionally a day of recognizing that we human beings are a pretty wretched bunch, each one of us. If we're ever going to change, we have to look honestly at where we are now. So on Ash Wednesday, in some churches, the people come together to worship and to have the sign of the cross made on their foreheads with ashes, usually made from burning the palm branches from last Palm Sunday.

As the sign is made, these words are spoken: "Remember that from dust thou art, and to dust thou shalt return." It's a way of admitting that God made us and that God will determine when we die—so he determines everything else that happens in between. Once we see that, we can give ourselves up to God and let him work with us to get a little further out of that wretched state.

We don't suggest that you have your own ash ceremony! But perhaps you could set the day aside in one of these ways:

- Wear a cross to remind you that Jesus died to save us from having to die forever because of our sin.
- Fast from something for one day, something you'll really miss, like gum or dessert.
- Carry a little mirror in your pocket as a reminder that you are entering a season of looking closely at yourself.

As the season of Lent begins, look at what you need to work on for the next forty days. Go back to the results of **Check Yourself Out** and come up with a simple plan for working with God to improve in that area. You'll want to include the four things Christians who observe Lent try to do:

- Practice a discipline, like reading the Bible every day.
- Give to the needy.
- Get rid of what separates you from God.
- Fast or do some form of self-denial so you can focus.

Below are some suggested plans. Feel free to use the one that's appropriate for you, or with the help of your mom or dad or your Sunday school teacher or pastor, design one that's exactly right in your case. Keep in mind that this is not a plan for punishing yourself—it's a program for realizing where you're drifting to and finding out how you can make your way back—you *and* God, that is.

If the area you need to work on is relationships, try this:

- **Discipline:** Read about the best relationships in the Bible, either using a translation of the Bible you can understand easily or a Bible storybook. Those would include Abraham and Lot, David and Jonathan, Ruth and Naomi, Jesus and his disciples, Jesus with Mary and Martha and Lazarus, Paul and Timothy.

You can set up a schedule for yourself on your calendar so you can study one set of friends a week during Lent (leaving out the last week). See if those Bible people set an example for how you should treat the people in your life.

- **Giving:** Decorate a container, such as a jar or a small box, and either leave it open or put a slit in the top. Gather up all your change (from piggy banks, couch cushions, etc.) and have it converted to pennies. Keep the pennies near your container. Every time someone does or says something positive or encouraging to you, put a penny of thanks in the container.

By Easter, you'll have a nice chunk of change to put in the offering plate or to give to your little sister who loves pennies or to the man collecting money for charity in front of the grocery store. It will surprise you how much nicer you are to other people when you have proof of how nice they are to you.

- **Getting rid of separation:** Pray every morning that God will help you improve your relationships with other people. Name them by name. Be specific about what your problems are with them. After you pray—every morning—listen.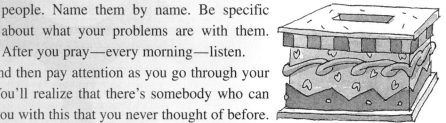

And then pay attention as you go through your day. You'll realize that there's somebody who can help you with this that you never thought of before. You'll find yourself thinking, *Oh, I really shouldn't say that—it always starts a fight.* You can also ask your parents or other adults for help. Ask the people you're trying to get along better with for help, or even read *The Buddy Book,* which has all kinds of suggestions for you.

- **Fasting:** Instead of giving up Gummi Bears or sodas, try giving up something that interferes with your getting along with people—something like gossiping, talking back, being sarcastic, teasing, or name calling. It's a whole lot harder to stop saying "Shut up!" than it is to deny yourself Sweet Tarts for forty days, but you're going to be so much better for it by Easter Day—and your new behavior will probably continue.

If the area you need to work on is responsibility, try this:

- **Discipline:** Read about the people in the Bible who carried out their responsibilities to the letter even when they didn't necessarily want to. You can use either a translation of the Bible you can understand easily or a Bible storybook. The characters would include Noah, Abraham and Isaac, Samuel, Esther, Daniel, Paul.

You can set up a schedule for yourself on your calendar so you can study one story a week during Lent (leaving out the last week). See if those Bible people set an example for how you can do the things you're supposed to do, even if they aren't the most fun things in life.

- **Giving:** Decorate a container, such as a jar or a small box, and either leave it open or put a slit in the top. Gather up all your change (from piggy banks, couch cushions, etc.) and have it converted to pennies. Keep the pennies near your container. Every time someone does something that affects your life in a good way, even though it costs that person time or money or aggravation, put a penny of thanks in the container (that would include your mom doing your laundry, your dad helping you with your math homework, your sister taking your turn with the dishes).

By Easter, you'll have money to put in the offering plate or to give to that sister who did your dishes. It will surprise you how paying attention to how responsible other people are will make you more responsible too.

- **Getting rid of separation:** Pray every morning that God will help you improve your sense of responsibility. Name the things you put off or don't do because you hate doing them. Be specific about the problems your procrastination creates. After you pray—every morning—listen. And then pay attention as you through your day.

You'll realize that there's somebody who can help you with this that you never thought of before. You'll find yourself thinking, *If I don't do this, it's going to make things harder for somebody else.* You can also ask your parents or other adults for help. Ask the people you're letting down for help, or even read *The Blurry Rules Book,* which has all kinds of suggestions for you.

- **Fasting:** Instead of giving up ice cream or popcorn, try giving up an activity that you would rather do than your chores or your homework— something like watching afternoon TV or talking on the phone before your homework is done or playing computer games. It's a lot easier to carry out your responsibilities when you don't have something else to do. You're going to be pretty responsible by Easter Day—and your new behavior will probably continue.

If the area you need to work on is self-discipline, try this:

- **Discipline:** Read about self-disciplined people in the Bible, the ones who avoided temptation. You can use either a translation of the Bible you can understand easily or a

Bible storybook. Those people would include Joseph (when he was tempted by Potiphar's wife), Balaam, Job, David sparing Saul's life, Micaiah, and Jesus.

You can set up a schedule for yourself on your calendar so you can study one story a week during Lent (leaving out the last week). See if those Bible people set an example for how you can get yourself in gear when nobody else is there to do it for you or would know the difference if you didn't.

- **Giving:** Decorate a container, such as a jar or a small box, and either leave it open or put a slit in the top. Gather up all your change (from piggy banks, couch cushions, etc.) and have it converted to pennies. Keep the pennies near your container. Every time you see someone automatically doing what they're supposed to, without any prompting from anybody—or you see someone resisting temptation—put a penny of thanks in the container.

That would include things like somebody leaving the last cookie in the box for the next person, your little brother brushing his teeth without being told, your dad getting up early to do devotions before he goes to work. By Easter, you'll have a pile of change to put in the offering plate or to buy your little brother a cool toothbrush. It will surprise you how paying attention to how self-disciplined other people are will make you more self-disciplined.

- **Getting rid of separation:** Pray every morning for God to help you be more self-disciplined. Name the things you do that you shouldn't do and the things you don't do that you should. Be specific about how you feel when you're slacking off. After you pray—every morning—listen. And then pay attention as you go through your day.

You'll realize that there's somebody who can help you with this that you never thought of before. You'll find yourself thinking, *I oughta get up and do this because nobody else should have to make me.* You can also ask your parents or other adults for help. Ask the people who always have to bug you to do things, or even read *The It's MY Life Book,* which has all kinds of suggestions for you.

- **Fasting:** Rather than denying yourself peanut M&Ms or McDonald's french fries, try giving up a bad habit. You'll probably need someone to help monitor you, since a habit is usually something you do without even realizing it. Do you bite your nails? Pick your nose? Crack your knuckles? Yeah, it's easier to push aside the Happy Meal than it is to stop chewing on your cuticles. But by Easter Day, that habit will be gone, and you'll be a more self-disciplined person—one who can focus more on the habits God wants you to have.

Holy Week

Starting with the Sunday before Easter, we enter a week called Holy Week, which is the last week that Jesus spent on earth in human form. It was an important time in his ministry, so it deserves special attention from us. If you are aware each day in the week of how close you're getting to Resurrection Day, Easter is going to mean more to you than it ever has before.

Palm Sunday

Read Mark 11:1–10 about Jesus' wonderful entrance into Jerusalem.

If your church hands out palm branches on this day, hang up yours in your room or make a cross out of it to pin to your shirt for the rest of the day. If your church doesn't carry out that tradition, pick your own palm leaf or other kind of branch and keep it in your room through the week to remind you that Jesus entered Jerusalem in triumph that day, just as he's entering you more and more all the time.

Break your fast for today (unless you've been fasting from a bad habit, in which case, treat yourself to a banana split or something). It's a way to rejoice in the knowledge that Jesus went to Jerusalem—for you.

Maundy or Holy Thursday

Read Mark 14:12–26 about the last supper Jesus had with his disciples on the night before he died.

Ask if your family can have what's called a Seder meal, which is a version of the Passover meal that Jesus was observing with his friends that night. If you want to go all the way with your Seder meal, there are books available that will show you how, or you can cruise the Internet for info. But if you and your family want to keep it simple, you can include these traditions:

- Put candles on the table that mean something to your family—maybe the ones you used during Advent or the candles you received when you were baptized.
- Add a centerpiece to represent the Lamb of God—even if it's a little ceramic piece.
- Serve foods that are symbols of the Israelites' leaving Egypt. Bitter herbs like horseradish, radishes, onions, or dill pickles symbolize the bitter suffering of the chosen people in slavery. We, too, suffer until we are freed from sin.
- Unleavened bread, such as crackers or tortillas, reminds us that the Jews left Egypt in a hurry and didn't have time to use yeast to bake their bread. It reminds us that Jesus may come when we least expect him.
- Lamb (if your family doesn't care for lamb, you can use turkey or chicken) represents God delivering the Jews from slavery by the use of the blood of the lamb placed over their doors so that their firstborn sons would be spared. It also reminds us that we don't have to make blood sacrifices, because Jesus is our Passover lamb—he already made the sacrifice of himself.
- Green vegetables symbolize springtime and the miracle of rebirth, not only of the earth but also of us as we've practiced our Lenten disciplines.
- Boiled egg gets harder instead of softer when it cooks. It symbolizes that the Israelites became strong in faith by patiently going through suffering. We can too.
- Grape juice represents the blood of Christ for us, as wine represented joy and life to the Jews.
- Set an extra place for a guest—the Lord Jesus.
- Begin by lighting the candles and blessing the feast.
- During the meal, be reverent, as you would be if Jesus were indeed sharing the supper with you. Finish with a prayer of thanksgiving.

It's also traditional to have a foot washing on Holy or Maundy Thursday, because Jesus washed the feet of his friends at that last supper (John 13:1–17). You can do that with your family or friends.

- Prepare a basin (like a dishpan) with warm water (no need to use soap, since this is symbolic) and have some towels on hand.
- Sit in a circle and ask each person to wash the feet of someone else in the group, until everyone's feet have been bathed. As the washing is done, the person doing the washing can say how he or she would like to serve the other person and why, or there can be silence while everyone prays silently. There might be giggling at first, but most people end up loving the ceremony and really getting into it.

Good Friday

This is the day Jesus died on the cross. It is the saddest of all the holy days, which doesn't mean you have to walk around weeping. But there are some things you can do to honor Christ on this day.

- Read the story of the arrest and the crucifixion, either in a Bible storybook or one of these Gospels: Matthew 26:36–27:61; Mark 14:32–15:47; Luke 22:39–23:56.

- Wear a cross, as you may have done on Ash Wednesday.
    - Try not to party today. This wouldn't be the day to have your birthday celebration or hold an Easter egg hunt.
        - Do quiet things in the afternoon if you can, like read or draw or go to your favorite alone spot. It's a way of showing respect for what Jesus went through for us.

Holy Saturday

In the early years after Jesus ascended into heaven, the first Christians thought he was going to return very soon, and they came to believe that it would be at the time of the celebration of his Resurrection—Easter. So a tradition began of keeping an all-night vigil—or watch—the night before Easter so they would be awake when he appeared. Jesus said no one knows when that will happen, but the tradition has become a symbol for always being ready and watchful for Christ.

Chances are pretty good that your mom and dad aren't going to let you stay up all night the night before Easter, even if it is to wait for Jesus! But here's a version of the Easter vigil that might meet with parental approval.

- Set up a special, quiet place for waiting, either alone or with members of your family or friends who understand the purpose of keeping a vigil. It can be at your front window or by the back door, in your room or outside on a porch or in a tent.
- You'll want to have something in your special place that will symbolize your keeping a light on for Jesus—candles (with permission), a lantern, a small lamp, or even a flashlight or a tiki torch if you're keeping your vigil outside.
- When adults keep a vigil, they usually sit silently or pray, but that might be a little hard for you since you're still in that always-have-to-be-moving stage of your life. So plan some quiet things to do—songs to sing, topics to talk about (everybody tells what they have learned

through Lenten discipline or what they would want Jesus to think of them if he did come tonight). You can even plan a snack.

- Start your vigil at dusk and continue until bedtime. Know as you drift off to sleep that when you wake up, it will be Easter. The Jesus you waited for will be there.

Easter Sunday

Most churches and Christian families have sacred traditions they practice on Easter Sunday—and even some not so sacred but fun (which God enjoys too!). It's fine to dig into an Easter basket full of candy to celebrate the breaking of your fast, and it's definitely okay to have an Easter egg hunt, the eggs symbolizing the new birth you're experiencing as you get closer and closer to Jesus. (Think of the shell as a tomb from which life springs.)

But it's also important to keep Jesus and his Resurrection in focus, because the Resurrection is central to what it means to be a Christian. God raised Jesus from the dead to show us that if we believe in him, we too can live forever (though not our earthly form) in perfect union with him. Here are some ways to help you keep that focus:

- If you haven't stayed up too late the night before, set your alarm for the time the sun's supposed to come up (the newspaper or the Weather Channel will tell you exactly when that will be). As you sip your juice, watch the sun come up and imagine what it must have been like at the empty tomb that first Easter Day. Read the story, either in a Bible storybook or in Matthew 28:1–10, Mark 16:1–11, Luke 24:1–12, or John 20:1–23.

If your family is really into it, you could assign parts (a few days before so people can practice) and read it as a drama using a narrator for the general part. If you have little kids in your family, you could make paper-bag puppets to represent the players and do a puppet presentation of the first Easter for them.

- Have a special Easter breakfast before church, maybe with some Easter lilies on the table, which are symbols of life and remind us of the white robes people wear when they are baptized at Easter. The menu could include eggs, a food the early Christians often used during the Lenten fast, and hot cross buns, which are glazed buns with a cross marked on top. (You can buy these in a bakery or help make them. If you can't find a recipe, look in a British or an Austrian cookbook.)

- Wear the best clothes you have. They don't have to be new—although that's fun—as long as you think of dressing up to the hilt as symbolic of taking off old ways of life and putting on the new way of Christ.
- Make a jelly-bean bag for each of your family members and maybe your friends too. Use the following colors:

  - One red one for Christ's blood
  - One green one for new life
  - One yellow one for the light of God's love
  - One orange one for the edge of night, which that light brightens for us
  - One black one to remind us of the sins from which Jesus has saved us
  - One white one for the purity of Jesus
  - One purple one for the hours of sorrow and the forty days of Lent
  - One pink one for the sunrise—our new tomorrow

You can either tell people what the colors mean or slip a note in that explains the symbolism (decorated with your creativity!).

Talking to God About It

Dear_____ (however you like to address our Father),
All this talk about Lent is really different for me, but I want to give it a try. Will you help me set my mind to please you as I prepare for Easter? The things I've checked off are the things I need the most help with:

_____ Not thinking of Lent as just a time to dye eggs and pick out which chocolate bunny I want in my basket

_____ Being honest with myself about what I need to work on during Lent

_____ Being able to carry through on those things I commit to do until Easter, since I have a habit of starting things I never finish

_____ Not thinking of Lenten disciplines as things only non-Protestants do

_____ Not giving up because my family isn't into what I'm doing or my friends think I'm a freak.

_____ Knowing that you're going to be right there with me, helping me, because you're the whole reason I'm doing it

_____ Coming to you if I do fall behind and picking up where I left off instead of giving up

_____ Not getting cranky about giving things up—because this is going to bring me closer to you

Thank you, God, for making the biggest sacrifice of all. I love you.

The biggest—and I mean the BIGGEST—temptation I ever faced was …

The Feast of Pentecost – A Birthday Celebration

You will receive power when the Holy Spirit
comes on you; and you will be my witnesses.
Acts 1:8

Do you ever get the feeling that when it comes to church, everything's kind of a chore?

You have to get up early when it's not even a school day.

You have to wear nice clothes—and it's the weekend! Hello!

In Sunday school, you study the same old Bible stories that you could probably recite in your sleep—and you might get a chance to demonstrate that, since the whole class is a snore.

In church, you're supposed to put money in the collection plate, even if you don't have very much to begin with. The sermon can sometimes be long, which is a drag, especially when your stomach is growling because you barely had time to choke down a Pop-Tart before you left the house. And that one lady in the choir—it's definitely a chore to listen to her voice: she sounds like a cat having its tail pulled.

If that were all there was to being a Christian, it *would* be a job—the worst job on the planet. It isn't—but the fact remains that it sometimes feels that way. You know, when you are thinking, *If I have to play an angel in one more Christmas pageant or hide one more Easter egg for the primary class to find, I'm going to scream!*

That's why God sent the Holy Spirit on the Day of Pentecost—because it's the Holy Spirit who makes our faith in God real to us. He acts in ways we can recognize to show us the presence of Jesus and the love and grace of God. Without his inspiration, everything related to God can start feeling like one more "thing" you have to endure.

The Feast of Pentecost is the holy day set aside to help us remember that Jesus sent the Holy Spirit to us and remind us that he's always there. It's a pretty big day in the Christian year. Without it, we would end up doing a lot of yawning in church.

Let's take a closer look at it.

How Is This a God Thing?

Even though we celebrate the coming of the Holy Spirit on the Day of Pentecost with a feast, that same Spirit has always been present in the world.

The first verses in the Bible tell us, "In the beginning God created the heavens and the earth. Now the earth was formless and empty, darkness was over the surface of the deep, and the Spirit of God was hovering over the waters" (Genesis 1:1–2).

Throughout the Old Testament, we see the mysterious Spirit of God inspiring people, giving them the power to do things they couldn't have done otherwise. Israel's leaders—from Moses to Joshua, and then the judges, and finally from David to Solomon—all received their wisdom and courage and power as gifts because they had the Spirit of God in them.

The best example in the Old Testament is the prophets, who obviously spoke and acted with a power that wasn't their own. Isaiah, Elijah, and Ezekiel weren't your run-of-the-mill people. They were Spirit-filled, and everybody knew it!

In the New Testament, from the minute Jesus began his ministry, nobody could deny that the Holy Spirit was on him. Look at all the examples from the Gospels:

- The Spirit of God spoke when Jesus was baptized (Matthew 3:13–17).
- It was the Spirit who sent Jesus out to the wilderness to be tempted by Satan (Mark 1:12).
- The Spirit came upon those who were released from demons by Jesus (Matthew 12:28).
- The Spirit of the Lord was on Jesus when he stood up in the synagogue in Nazareth to read from Holy Scripture (Luke 4:18).

Before he left the disciples, Jesus promised them that they weren't going to be alone, that he was going to ask the Father to give them another Counselor to be with them forever. It was that Counselor—the Holy Spirit—who would live in them and allow them to continue to see and hear Jesus and know what God wanted them to do (John 14:15–21).

And that's exactly what happened. The apostles were gathered together in one place when suddenly a sound "like the blowing of a violent wind" came from heaven and filled the whole house (Acts 2:2). They saw what looked like tongues of fire that separated and stopped at each one of them. At that moment, they were filled with the Holy Spirit, just as Jesus had promised. Their first sign? They all began to speak in other languages, because the Spirit gave them that power.

Naturally that created quite a ruckus, and a bunch of Jewish people from various nations came running. They were surprised. Surprised? They were flabbergasted! Because each one of them heard people speaking in his or her own language, declaring the wonders of God (Acts 2:1–12).

Granted, some of the people who saw this went away thinking the apostles had had too much wine (even though it was only nine in the morning). But many of them had to wonder, *What does this mean?* (Acts 2:13).

Peter stood up and explained it to them, going way back to the prophet Joel, who had prophesied that God would pour out his Spirit on all people, and then telling them about the things Jesus had done and said. Right then, more than a few of those people wanted to be baptized and become part of what the apostles were living (Acts 2:37–39).

So the Day of Pentecost is important to Christians. When you think about it, it's kind of like the birthday of the Christian church, because on that day the first ministers were ordained by God and started to preach and gather people together for fellowship and for the breaking of bread and for prayer (Acts 2:42–47).

It wasn't the church you may consider boring and a big interruption of your Sunday morning sleep. It was a group of people who were filled with the Holy Spirit, and they were able to do amazing things. We can too, because we have the Holy Spirit just as they did. He is always right here with us—living in us. Sometimes it takes a reminder like a birthday feast to help us see what's there for us—what God wants us to have.

What does the Holy Spirit do? What is his mission?

- The Holy Spirit points us to Jesus.
- The Holy Spirit teaches us.
- The Holy Spirit helps us understand the Bible so we can use it in our lives.

We're only human. We need the evidence of a living Jesus that the Holy Spirit brings to our lives.

Girlz WANT TO KNOW

✿ *LILY: Okay—hold everything. Does celebrating Pentecost mean I have to speak in tongues? I don't think I can do that!*

Not at all! The ability to speak in tongues is only one of the gifts of the Holy Spirit mentioned in the Bible. There are bunches, and all of us have at least one. (For lots more about spiritual gifts, read *The Uniquely Me Book*.) The Feast of Pentecost is a day to celebrate what the Holy Spirit is doing in you and in your church as a whole, with all of its people and their different gifts. By the way, in some churches, nobody speaks in tongues, and the Holy Spirit is still very much with them. It's just one piece of evidence—among many.

✿ *RENI: I pray to God the Father, I follow Jesus' teachings, and I know he saved me. I'm doing just fine with that. I think if I add the Holy Spirit, it's gonna get pretty crowded in my head. Do I have to do the Holy Spirit thing?*

Actually, Reni, the Holy Spirit is there to connect you to God and to Jesus. Being disconnected from the Spirit is like being cut off on the phone. Suddenly, you're not talking to God anymore. You're not hearing proof that Jesus is there for you. You're out of the loop! Besides, don't worry about things getting crowded in your head. The Spirit isn't just in your thoughts—he's in the core of you, doing things you're not even conscious of. The more aware you are of his presence, the more you'll realize that God loves you and approves of you because you accept Jesus—and the better your life will be.

✿ *ZOOEY: Um, what if I don't feel the Holy Spirit—you know, like I don't know for sure he's there? Does that mean I'm not a Christian?*

Absolutely not! If you know that Jesus is the son of God and that his life and death all happened so you can have eternal life—and you're living like you believe that—you are a Christian. If being a Christian has never filled you with awe and wonder, with strength and courage, or with peace and joy, that's probably because you haven't been shown how exciting it all can be. Some of that is out of your control right now because you have to go to the church your parents or friends take you to. But most of it is between you and God. Here's how you can get connected so you will feel more like you're on the adventure God has planned for you, with the Holy Spirit as your companion.

- Try a different way of praying. Go out by yourself somewhere and talk out loud to God or sing your prayers. Do it loud and huge. Dance if you feel like it. Enjoy being in the big, big presence of God.
- Get some praise music CDs or tapes and listen to them while you're doing chores or hanging out. Sing along—or use headphones if somebody you live with complains. The psalms were songs sung to God, so music and the Holy Spirit have been partners for a long time. Tap into that.
- Write letters to God the way you would to a friend you miss. Invite him to be there next to you. He'll show up—through the Spirit.

- Keep your eyes—and ears—open for the Holy Spirit in the beautiful things around you. Watch for sunsets and sunrises, if you can haul yourself out of bed that early. Check out the scenery around you. Whether it's mountains, oceans, farm fields, or wildflowers along the highway, it's a God-thing. Sit silently on your front porch or at your window and listen in the early morning or evening. Notice how beautiful the sounds are when you tune in. It's God out there showing off his Spirit.
- Talk to people you know who are living the Christian way of life and ask them about the Holy Spirit. They'll have stories to tell. Soon you'll have yours too—because mostly all you have to do is ask God to show you, and he will. Why on earth would he keep it a secret?

✿ *SUZY: I don't know if I should celebrate Pentecost. I mean, I haven't had a big conversion experience where tongues of flame came down. I just believe in Jesus.*

Not everybody has a vision of flames when they first come to believe in Christ. Some, like you, are lucky enough to just know. But that doesn't mean the quiet Christians like you shouldn't celebrate the fact that the Holy Spirit came to the apostles and equipped them to spread the word about Jesus. If it weren't for that, you wouldn't have that still, small voice in you who says God's there. And even quiet people can celebrate!

✓ CHECK Yourself OUT

Now that you know what we're talking about when we say "Holy Spirit" and before we go on to how to celebrate him—let's find out how you sense the presence of God's Spirit. This is not a test to find out how good you are—or how rotten! This is intended to help you see how to get your best sense of God being near you in spirit. That'll determine how you can best celebrate too, as you'll see further on.

Go through each of these three lists and put a check mark next to each item that makes you feel close to God. If that's too hard for you, check off those things that make you feel happy or peaceful and never drive you nuts or bore you to tears.

_____ watching a storm
_____ seeing a sunset or a sunrise
_____ looking at the ocean
_____ feeling small beside a mountain
_____ walking through a field of wildflowers
_____ hearing rain on the roof
_____ listening to a fire crackle
_____ hearing waves crash on the shore
_____ seeing light stream through clouds
_____ looking up at the stars

_____ seeing a baby smile
_____ holding a puppy
_____ being at the table with the whole family
_____ laughing with people
_____ singing with a group
_____ hugging Mom or Dad
_____ snuggling in next to somebody
_____ holding somebody's hand
_____ being reunited with somebody who's been gone
_____ hearing Mom's or Dad's voice when things get scary

_____ reading the Bible or a Bible story
_____ understanding something in Sunday school class or in church
_____ reading about great Christians
_____ praying alone
_____ daydreaming

_____ having a talk with somebody who really knows God

_____ wearing a cross

_____ writing in a diary or journal

_____ lighting a candle

_____ taking Communion

Count up the number of checks you have in each list and write the numbers in the slots below:

_____LIST 1   _____LIST 2   _____LIST 3

If you had more checks in list A, you probably sense the presence of the Holy Spirit most when you're in the natural world. Things like big waterfalls of light shooting out of the clouds make you think of God or make you feel peaceful or give you goose bumps. You probably take in a lot of your information about the world through your five senses, so that's one of the main ways God reaches out to you.

If you want to feel the Holy Spirit more, spend your quiet time outside or near a window where you can look out and see beautiful things in creation. Find or draw some nature pictures to put up in your room to remind you how close God is. Ask if you can pick some flowers to put in your room. Collect leaves and wildflowers and press them (there are lots of books that can show you how to do that).

When you're doing those things—or collecting rocks or shells or checking out how many different kinds of birds you can see—talk to God about what you're seeing, hearing, smelling, tasting, and touching. He put it all there for you to enjoy. Letting you feel the presence of the Holy Spirit through those things is his way of enjoying it with you.

If you had more checks in list B, you usually feel the Holy Spirit when you're with people you love and when your emotions are high. Crying, laughing, hugging, talking—those are like little doors opening up for you to see God. You probably take in a lot of your information about the world through your relationships and emotions, so that's one of the main ways God reaches out to you.

If you want to feel the Holy Spirit more, make sure you're in a Sunday school class or youth group where you can hang out with other Christian kids a lot. Talk to your mom and dad or another adult who is all about God and share your thoughts and feelings and questions with that person. When you're praying alone, talk to God—even out loud. Get an image of God in your mind. It might even help you to have a painting or drawing of Jesus—what an artist thinks Jesus looked like, anyway—in your room as a reminder of how real God is.

And when you're talking to God, let your emotions come on out. God made those tears, your giggle, and those hairs that stand up on the back of your neck when you're mad. He wants to help you use them—through his Spirit.

If you had more checks in list C, you probably know the presence of the Holy Spirit through the thoughts that come to you, and those thoughts may come through something you read or a discussion you've heard or even in your quiet time. Pay attention to your thoughts. If they go against what Jesus taught, you can toss those babies out. But if not—if they seem to be telling you something about God—that could be the Spirit whispering in your active brain. You probably take in most of your information about the world in an intellectual way (chances are you're a good student and you like to read and learn new stuff), so why wouldn't God show himself to you that way?

If you want to be more aware of the Holy Spirit, have a grown-up help you find a good Bible study that's appropriate for your age group. Ask Christians you respect some questions and listen to their answers. Read about Christians from the past who made a difference. When you pray, imagine yourself having a deep discussion with God.

The Holy Spirit may not spell all the answers out for you right then, but if you're paying attention, you'll find them as time goes on—in the things you read, the things wise people say to you, and the thoughts that spring suddenly into your head. They aren't from out of nowhere. They're from the Spirit.

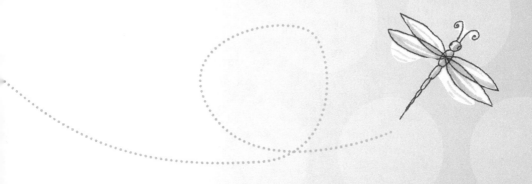

Just Do It

We know you have this part down, but just in case—you don't have to do all of these activities. They're suggestions to get you thinking—and celebrating!

- Break out that holy days calendar again. The Feast of Pentecost is fifty days after Easter Sunday, so start counting. When you label it, you might want to use red, the traditional color for Pentecost. It symbolizes the tongues of flame that descended above the heads of Jesus' followers as they received the Holy Spirit.
- The Day of Pentecost is a great day to deck yourself out in red. Besides being the traditional color, it's bright and festive and puts you in a high-spirited mood. Go for it—socks to hair gizzie!
- Have a party! It doesn't have to be elaborate. It could be dinner with your family after church or a backyard get-together with some of your friends. Since all languages could be understood on the Day of Pentecost, include things from various cultures. Could you have a piñata, filled with Pentecost trinkets—like fireballs (the kind you eat), Dove candy bars, and those party horns you blow through to represent wind? How about fortune cookies with Scripture verses telling of the Day of Pentecost? Maybe you could have the guests try to put them in order without consulting a Bible.

And what about a menu of Italian pizza, Mexican nachos, and French fries? If your mom's willing, this would be the perfect occasion for baked Alaska, which is a dessert that arrives at the table on fire!

- It's the birthday of the church, so give it your best wishes (or should we say, prayers). Make a birthday cake for the church and serve it to your family. What a cool time to invite your Sunday school teacher or your youth pastor or whomever shares God with you. Make or buy a gift for your church. Put up some red streamers or a couple of red balloons. If you're feeling artsy, you could incorporate some flames in there (paper, of course).

- If you want to have your own private observance of the Day of Pentecost, either instead of or in addition to a gathering of friends, why not choose something that fits your best way of feeling the presence of the Holy Spirit?.

- **List A people might enjoy going on a prayer picnic.** Pack your most to-die-for snacks and go to your favorite private place or special spot (letting somebody know where you are). You might want to take some drawing supplies along so you can sketch what you see that brings you close to the Spirit. Or write a poem or bask in the sun. It's just you and God, bathed in the Spirit.

- **List B people might prefer to throw a party.** But in case you do want to do something by yourself, make a memento (like a souvenir) of Pentecost to give to someone. Could it be a card with verses about the Day of Pentecost on it? A bookmark? A holy days calendar? A tea party on a tray to share with someone? Don't forget the hug. That will seal the celebration for you.

- **List C people may want to find a quiet, and preferably sunny, place to curl up with a book that will set their souls on fire—or at least inspire them a little!** Have you read *The Lion, the Witch, and the Wardrobe* (the first book in the Chronicles of Narnia by C. S. Lewis)? Madeline L'Engle's *A Wrinkle in Time*? Any books by Lee Roddy, Sigmund Brouwer, Bill Myers, Robert Elmer, Paul McCusker, Dave and Netta Jackson, or … Nancy Rue? Include a cup of hot chocolate or your favorite soda and a snack (red hots are great for Pentecost. Or how about barbecued potato chips?). Then read, munch, and let yourself get jazzed by what you read. There is nothing like reading about people who have taken the same power given to the apostles and letting it work in their lives. Chances are, you'll want to get up and do something amazing for God when you're through.

However you choose to celebrate the Feast of Pentecost, remember that the whole season of Pentecost now stretches before you, until the first Sunday in Advent (you remember that …) You can mark it in green, because it's another of those ordinary seasons like Epiphany. We won't outline something for you to do every day of the Pentecost season (yikes!), but there are some things you can think about and read about and learn from over these next six months:

- Jesus showing his holiness to Peter and James and John on the mountaintop
- Jesus preaching the Sermon on the Mount, which is full of stuff for us to live by
- Jesus healing the sick
- Jesus performing some pretty miraculous ... well ... miracles!
- Jesus taking his disciples aside and teaching them special things

When you think about it, those aren't ordinary activities. These next six months would be a good time to look at how not so ordinary your life is when you live it full-out for God. Here are some things you can do to help you remember that during the season of Pentecost:

- Start keeping a journal or a diary if you aren't already doing that. Write about snippets of your day that made you laugh, cry, get mad, or think.
- Plant some seeds and watch them grow. You can call it your Pentecost garden.
- Begin a project that could take a while to finish, doing it in small steps. It could be a large jigsaw puzzle, learning how to embroider and making a sampler, reading all of the Chronicles of Narnia—the possibilities are endless. When you're finished—before Advent— you'll be able to see how the ordinary days and their ordinary tasks add up to a whole.

- Set a goal for yourself and plan how you're going to achieve it by Advent. (You might need some help with this one.) Your goal can be anything that's going to help you serve God and his church—from learning how to play some praise songs on the guitar so you can pitch in with the little kids' music program to conquering your shyness enough to join the youth group. And remember, the Holy Spirit will be with you.

Talking to God About It

Dear _____ (your favorite way of addressing our Father),

I'm getting ready to celebrate the Pentecost in some way, and the things I've checked off here are the things I need help with:

_____ *understanding the Holy Spirit*
_____ *believing I need to be aware of the Holy Spirit*
_____ *feeling the presence of the Holy Spirit*
_____ *getting inspired to celebrate the Pentecost*
_____ *not expecting too much of my family because I want to have a feast and they might not*
_____ *keeping it about the Spirit and not just a party*
_____ *following through with what I plan*
_____ *always knowing that you're there in Spirit, God, and not just on this one day*

And, God, thank you for sending the Holy Spirit, the Counselor, because I really need him to know that you're there to help me with absolutely everything in my life—like, for instance:

_____

_____

Most of all, God, please show me how you want me to work in the Spirit, spreading your Good News to everyone. It isn't a secret, I know. Please help me to share it without . . .

_____ *getting embarrassed.*
_____ *being too shy.*
_____ *embarrassing other people.*
_____ *being too pushy.*
_____ *losing interest in doing it.*

88

You're the best—Father, Son, and Holy Spirit. I hardly have words to describe you, but the ones I do have are:

_____

_____

Amen. Amen. AMEN!

The time I felt God was nearest to me was ...

God Bless America

**Be strong and let us fight bravely
for our people and the cities of our God.**
2 Samuel 10:12

So far we've talked about the holy days, the ones that obviously are all about God.

But there are other holidays during the year that you probably get just as jazzed about—like . . .

★ Memorial Day
★ the Fourth of July
★ Labor Day
★ Thanksgiving

Granted, the first things that come to your mind when you think about those celebrations are flags, picnics, parades, turkey, and mashed potatoes, and the ever-popular days off from school. Don't stop thinking about those things, for heaven's sake! But as you're revving up for fireworks, pumpkin pie, or a day at the lake, keep in mind that God blesses those patriotic holidays too. So it only makes sense to observe the sacred in them while you're pouring on the gravy or lighting your sparklers.

How Is This a God Thing?

A patriot is someone who loves his or her country, and there were plenty of patriots back in the Bible days. God created the nation of Israel—also referred to as Zion—to be his special people, and he wanted them to love the country he had given them. The psalms are full of patriots doing just that. Here's one good example: "He has set his foundation on the holy mountain; the LORD loves the gates of Zion. . . . Glorious things are said of you, O city of God" (Psalm 87:1, 3).

Out of love for their country, the biblical patriots prayed constantly for God to preserve and protect it. One psalmist prayed, "In your good pleasure make Zion prosper; build up the walls of Jerusalem" (Psalm 51:18).

Not only did they pray, but they also took action.

• David was constantly defending the land. If you read from 1 Samuel 17, when he takes down Goliath, all the way to 1 Chronicles 29, when he dies, you'll wonder if there was a month, a week, or a day even, when he wasn't involved in some kind of battle.

- Moses left the luxury of Pharaoh's court to rejoin his people.
- And let's not leave out the women. Deborah not only sent Barak and ten thousand men of Naphtali and Zebulun to defend Israel—she went with them.

All through the Old Testament we see God's people loving, building, preserving, and defending their land. God loved it that they did that, and he told them to celebrate over it as well. As part of his instructions to Moses, he said, "When you have entered the land the LORD your God is giving you as an inheritance and have taken possession of it and settled in it, take some of the firstfruits of all that you produce from the soil of the land the LORD your God is giving you and put them in a basket. Then go to the place the LORD your God will choose as a dwelling for his Name.... Place the basket before the LORD your God and bow down before him. And you ... shall rejoice in all the good things the LORD your God has given to you and your household" (Deuteronomy 26:1–2, 10–11).

God has blessed us with a great nation to live in as well. Even though it's easy to forget when we look at the way many Americans live, our country was founded in God's name, and its government was set up according to godly principles. Look at what the Pledge of Allegiance says: "one nation, under God, indivisible, with liberty and justice for all."

Just as God asked the people of Israel to rejoice in all the good things God had given them in their new land, so he wants us to do the same thing. We may not be proud of everything that happens in America, but we can be thankful for the same things God is proud of:

- the freedom to worship however we choose
- the freedom to go after whatever we think God wants us to do in our lives (as long as it doesn't trample on anyone else's freedom)
- protection from anyone who would try to take away those freedoms

Rejoice, then! Those are good things!

Just Do It

Your family probably has traditions for some of the patriotic holidays. If you'd like to weave a sacred thread into those traditions—if it isn't there already—here are some things you can do. (Remember—don't try to do them all. Just pick a few and rejoice in them to the hilt!)

Memorial Day

This is the day toward the end of May on which we honor all the men and women who have given their lives in service to their country. It's kind of hard to thank God that people had to die, but we can thank him that there were people who were willing to, so that we can still be free today. So perhaps you could include their memories in your family's celebration.

• Set an extra place or two at the picnic table for friends and family of years gone by who were patriots. If you have pictures of them or mementos that belonged to them, include them in the centerpiece.
• Name them by name when you ask the blessing, in thanksgiving for what they sacrificed.
• Drink a toast to them, everyone lifting those sodas high in their honor.
• Ask grown-ups in the group to tell you about those people.

Fourth of July

This is the day to say "Happy Birthday, America!" It marks the signing of the Declaration of Independence, the first step toward freedom for the United States. God had a hand in that to be sure! Perhaps you could include some of these things in your family's activities.

- Just as you used red for Pentecost, deck everything out in red, white, and blue, including yourself. Try to use God's showing off of those colors in there—blueberries, watermelon, red carnations, white daisies, strawberries.
- Since you'll be flying the flag, make a God banner to display as well. The stars and stripes are symbols for our country, so include God symbols on your banner—whatever represents a freedom-giving God for you.
- This is one of the most important days of the year to ask a blessing over your lunch or supper. Make it extra special. Have everyone hold hands and say what freedom he or she is thankful for before you pray or during the prayer.
- Bake a cake for America's birthday, but instead of singing "Happy Birthday," sing "God Bless America" or "My Country 'Tis of Thee" or "The Battle Hymn of the Republic."

Labor Day

This is the first Monday in September, the day for honoring people who work hard—which is just about every grown-up! Sometimes Labor Day gets overlooked because school is starting and the summer is winding down. But because the adults in your life work so that you can have food and shelter and an education as well as the fun stuff, God doesn't want you to overlook it. Why not make it a day when you show your adult family and friends how much you appreciate their labor?

- Offer to help get ready for any activities your family has planned—tidying up the yard for a barbecue, cleaning out the car for a day trip, hosing out the cooler for a picnic.

- If nothing has been planned, maybe you could be in charge of putting together a simple Labor Day celebration. Do what you can do comfortably, like make a pile of peanut butter and jelly sandwiches, mix up some lemonade, pour a bag of chips into a basket, spread out a blanket in the backyard or on the family room floor and—voilà!—instant picnic party. If you want to give your parents and other invited adults a lift, put their music on the stereo. Don't let them lift a finger to get things ready. They work hard all year—now it's your turn to do something.

- Put together a fun package for the adults you're honoring. Take a hunk of your allowance to the Dollar Store or be creative with what you can find around the house. You could include:
  → a couple of pieces of their favorite candy or gum.
  → a book of your favorite jokes—written and illustrated by you.
  → a toy to play with—a yo-yo, a whistle, a funky rubber animal that sticks out its tongue when you squeeze it.
  → a token of their favorite hobby—a fake worm for your dad who fishes, a packet of seeds for your grandmother who gardens, a toy motorcycle for your grandfather who has a Harley.
  → a thank-you card at each person's place at the table or picnic blanket.

- When it's time to ask a blessing, remember to thank God for jobs, for satisfying careers, for people who are willing to work hard to make life better for everyone.

- While you're eating, get the grown-ups talking by asking questions like, What was your first job? What has been your most fun job? What was the job you'd most like to forget? What's your favorite part of the work you do now? Kids in the group can describe their dream jobs.

Thanksgiving Day

Just about everybody in America celebrates this day in honor of the Pilgrims who sacrificed so much to settle in the New World we now call home.

Sometimes, though, it's overshadowed by that biggest of all holidays, Christmas, which is right on its heels. Before the leftover turkey is even gone, lights start going up on people's houses and Santa's ringing his bell in front of every store. The best way to make Thanksgiving a holy day is to keep God in the center of it, where he belongs. You might try some of these activities:

• Ask your mom or dad if you can read a psalm out loud at the dinner table. Pick one of these (or choose your own) and practice it until you can read it smoothly and with love. There are different translations of the Bible, and it's okay to pick the one that's easiest for you to read and understand. If you want, you can ask other members of the family to read verses too. This could happen before the dinner is served (as long as those mashed potatoes don't get cold!) or at the end when everyone is digesting and making room for pie. Some especially thankful ones are Psalm 8, 9, 19, 23, 24, 29, 46, 66, 67, 84, 93, 96, 98, 100, 104, 111, 113, 117, 121, 122, 126, 134, 136, 145, 148, 150.

- While you're having dinner, ask each person at the table to say what he or she is most thankful for now in his or her life. If everyone is comfortable with this, you might ask, "When did you see God this year?"
- If you know beforehand who's going to be at your Thanksgiving table (whether it's at your house, someone else's, or in a restaurant), make something for each person. It can be a card telling what makes you thankful about that person, or a favor that represents that (you're thankful that your sister helps you with your math, so you give her a new, sharpened pencil with an eraser that hasn't been used), or a drawing showing that thankful thing (your mom making brownies, your dad driving you to soccer practice). If your family has a camera you're allowed to use, you could take pictures of your family members doing what makes you most grateful to them and include that in your card or letter.
- Using that same photograph idea—or perhaps pictures from magazines—make a scrapbook to present to your family, displaying the things in your life that make you thankful. If there's someone who can't be with the family on Thanksgiving Day, you could send your book to that person.

Girlz WANT TO KNOW

♣ *LILY: On the Fourth of July, my little brother says, "Do we have to put God in everything? Why can't we just have a normal holiday?" What am I supposed to do with that?*

What your little brother doesn't realize is that God is already in everything! But it doesn't sound like now is the time to throw that in his face. You might tone down your display of enthusiasm a little and just share the God-ness of these holidays with the people who are open to it—for now, anyway. As time goes by, you can bring God more and more into the center of things, but slowly, in small steps. Meanwhile, there's probably nobody stopping you from keeping God at the center of you as you celebrate a normal holiday with your family.

✿ *KRESHA: I don't like war, and I don't want to celebrate it. It seems like the Fourth of July and Memorial Day are all about people going out and fighting. I like to go on picnics and see fireworks, but I don't want to talk about people dying in wars.*

Probably nobody really likes war, so when we celebrate patriotic holidays and honor the patriots, we aren't holding a feast for how great battles are. We're remembering the sacrifices and celebrating the freedom we have because of those people giving up their lives. It's not something we should forget—because the minute we do, that's the time we're wide open to having our freedoms taken away. But that doesn't mean your Memorial Day celebration has to look like a funeral. Celebrate the *lives* of those patriots, not their deaths. If you look carefully at the suggestions for Memorial Day under **Just Do It,** you'll see how that can work. If you still feel funky, say a silent prayer for them in the midst of your fun instead. God appreciates whatever you offer.

✿ *ZOOEY: I want to make thank-you cards to put at everybody's place at Thanksgiving, but my mom says, "Zooey, I've set a nice table, and I don't want you cluttering it up." I don't feel very thankful about that!*

No, you probably don't—but don't despair. You can still show your appreciation to people with wonderful handmade cards. Hand them out between dinner and dessert or tuck them into people's hands as they're leaving. We all have to compromise when we live in community with people, right?

✓ **CHECK Yourself OUT**

Now that you know what holy days are and have learned some ways to make them and all your holidays—and perhaps *all* your days—sacred, let's check where you are in your holiday 'tude. Put a star next to each statement below that you can honestly say you know is true.

_____ It's important to make God a big part of the holy days—and not just focus on things like presents and days off from school.

_____ The holy days are important for all Christians.

_____ Traditions, rituals, and sacraments are reminders of important God things that we can't always see and sometimes forget to think about.

_____ What we celebrate on holy days can stay with us all year long.

_____ If we want our holy days to be sacred, we're going to have to include God in the planning.

Count your stars and write your number here: _____

If your score is a 5—you get it. Pray, plan, celebrate, and enjoy the results all year. It's exciting how much you're going to learn.

If your score is 3 or 4, you're on the right track. Look at the items you didn't put a star by and pray about those. Maybe you'll even want to go back and read chapter 1 again. But don't think you're a lousy Christian who doesn't want to take time for God! Choose the holy day that most appeals to you right now and celebrate that one this year. Most of the time, having fun that's filled with meaning leads to wanting more fun that's filled with meaning.

If your score is 0, 1, or 2, don't toss this book in the trash! Put it away for a little while. Pray about why you're bummed out about or not interested in holy days. Talk to somebody who is interested. God will show you what's holding you back. You'll know when you come across this book again and have the urge to read it. Things usually don't happen until God knows you're ready. Meanwhile, enjoy the holidays and holy days as much as you can. God loves to see us in joy.

Talking to God About It

Dear _____ (your favorite name for God),

Thank you for giving us a country where we can be free and for providing holidays when we can focus on that. When it comes to those holidays, I especially love _____.

Please help me to make those days more sacred, more about you, in whatever way I can. To do that, I need special help with . . .

_____ compromising with what other people in my family want.

_____ not forgetting about it once I start swimming or gluing turkey feathers onto pine cones.

_____ making sure whatever I do is about you and not about me.

_____ not being angry or crushed if my mom or dad says, "No! You can't do that!"

And, God, please be in the hearts of those people in the world who aren't free and who can't worship you as they please and are put down and made to be miserable, especially the people in

_____.

If there is anything I can do for any person who is suffering from lack of freedom in any way, please show me. Help me always to be an American you can be proud of.

Amen.

One freedom I should NOT want to give up ... would be ...

_____

_____

_____

_____

_____

_____

_____

_____

_____

_____

Rough & Rugged Lily

Nancy Rue

If you liked *The Year
'Round Holiday Book*,
you'll love its fictional
companion *Rough &
Rugged Lily*

Chapter 1

This is gonna be way cool," Lily said.

She squirmed around under her seatbelt so she could see Suzy and Reni in the backseat. They were both nodding, and even in the darkness of the van, she could tell both pairs of dark eyes were shining with that kind of delight that appears only when something really neat is about to happen.

"I didn't think we'd get to do anything this big in *Junior* Youth Group," Reni said, the beads on her numerous braids clacking together as she shook her head. "I thought they only did stuff like camp-outs in the *Senior* group."

"Is it gonna be that big, I mean, really?" Suzy said.

Lily didn't have to be able to see her to know her eyebrows were coming together in a worry knot. She'd wondered how long it would take nervous little Suzy to start stressing about this — but Lily was ready for her.

"It's gonna be major big," Lily said. She loosened her seatbelt a little so she could get up on her knees and peer at her two friends over the seat.

"You heard them say this is gonna be total 'survival in the wild,'" Reni put in.

"But there's nothing to worry about. You saw those people who are gonna head it up — they're professionals. And besides, they're gonna be training us from now 'til March, which is — "

"Three months," Reni said.

"So it's gonna be fine." Lily gave her head of curly red hair a final nod. She could see Suzy nodding, too, though with less enthusiasm. Suzy wasn't a go-at-everything-full-blast person. Lily was already envisioning herself pitching a tent up in the Poconos, fully prepared to ward off an entire family of bears.

"I'm glad we've got three months to get ready," Reni said. "I'm gonna have to do some *major* talking to get my dad to fork over for all that camping equipment. Did you see all that stuff they had up there on the stage?"

"But they said we didn't have to buy all that," Suzy said. "They said we should just be looking in our garages and attics for stuff."

"My parents don't *have* stuff," Reni said. "They've never been camping in their lives!"

For the first time since they'd left the church parking lot, Lily turned to look at her father, who was driving the van — and probably writing his next lecture on C. S. Lewis in his head. As she looked at his slender, freckled hands on the steering wheel and his I'm-dreaming-of-*The-Chronicles-of-Narnia* eyes peering through the icy windshield, it occurred to Lily that she might have the same problem.

"Do *we* have any camping equipment around the house, Dad?" she said.

Dad pulled the van to a stop at a red light and looked at her as if he'd just realized she was in the car with him. "Do we have *what,* Lilliputian?" he said. The heater wasn't working too well in the van, and the "what" came out with a puff of frosty breath.

"Camping equipment," Lily said.

"Why?" Dad said. "Are you planning to run away from home?"

Lily rolled her eyes at Suzy and Reni, who giggled into their mittened hands. Dad had *so* not heard a word they'd been saying—and it didn't take a nuclear physicist to figure out that there wasn't so much as a tent stake anywhere *near* the Robbins' house.

"I'll ask Mom," she said. "I bet she camped before you guys got married."

Dad chuckled. "She tried to drag me out into the wild once, but I managed to escape."

That was good for more eye rolling.

"Ooh—look at *those* lights!" Reni said.

Reni was clearing a circle in the fog on the side window. Lily craned her neck to see what she was pointing at. It was pretty hard to miss. Somebody's yard was so lit up that it looked as if the sky had snowed twinkle lights.

"We saw that the other night," Suzy said. "My dad said he'd hate to see their electric bill."

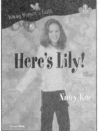

NIV Young Women of Faith Bible
GENERAL EDITOR SUSIE SHELLENBERGER

Designed just for girls ages 8-12, the *NIV Young Women of Faith Bible* not only has a trendy, cool look, it's packed with fun to read in-text features that spark interest, provide insight, highlight key foundational portions of Scripture, and more. Discover how to apply God's word to your everyday life with the *NIV Young Women of Faith Bible*.

Hardcover 0-310-91394-2
Softcover 0-310-70278-X
Slate Leather–Look™ 0-310-70485-5   **NEW!**
Periwinkle Leather–Look™ 0-310-70486-3   **NEW!**

Available now at your local bookstore!

Zonder**kidz**™

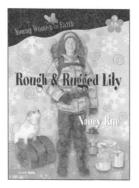

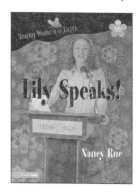
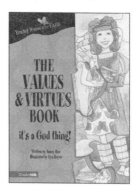

We want to hear from you. Please send your comments about this book to us in care of the address below. Thank you.

Zonder**kidz**™

Grand Rapids, MI 49530
www.zonderkidz.com